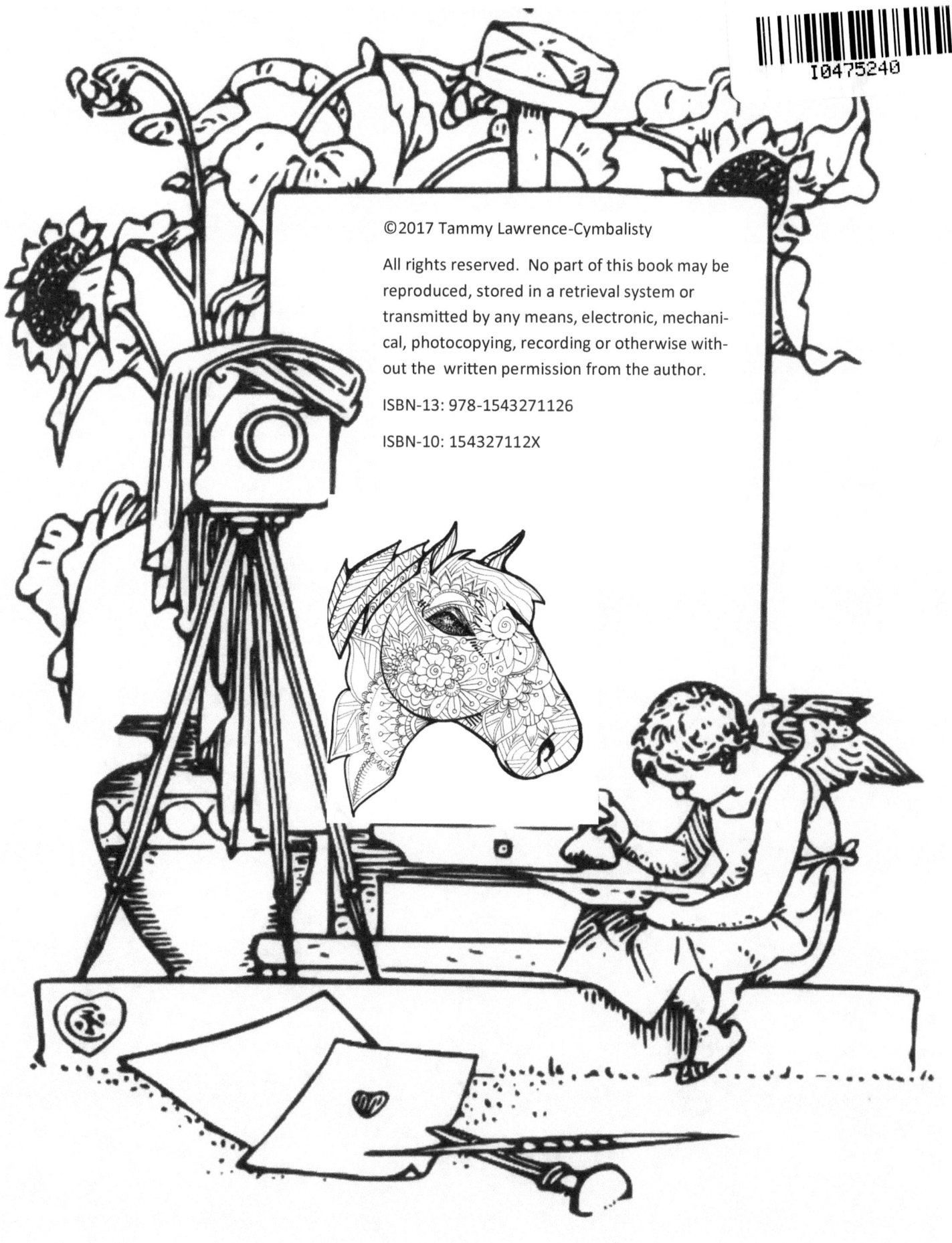

ISBN-13: 978-1543271126

ISBN-10: 154327112X

Welcome to I'm a Horse: My Chinese Zodiac Colouring Book.

Thank you so much for your purchase!

"People born within these date ranges can be said to have been born in the "Year of the Horse", while also bearing the following elemental signs:

Start date	End date	Heavenly branch
30 January 1930	16 February 1931	Metal Horse
15 February 1942	4 February 1943	Water Horse
3 February 1954	23 January 1955	Wood Horse
21 January 1966	8 February 1967	Fire Horse
7 February 1978	27 January 1979	Earth Horse
27 January 1990	13 February 1991	Metal Horse
12 February 2002	31 January 2003	Water Horse
31 January 2014	18 February 2015	Wood Horse
17 February 2026	5 February 2027	Fire Horse
4 February 2038	23 January 2039	Earth Horse

Source: https://en.wikipedia.org/wiki/Horse_(zodiac)

The five Horses hold different themes to their personality. These themes and characteristics are said to be based on the elements. You'll find some of them listed in the final pages of this book along with a meditation to help you further connect with your Zodiac Animal.

I suggest placing a piece of paper behind the pictures (you could also choose waxed paper) to prevent bleed-through. The pictures have a page between them to help with this.

You'll find lots of areas in the pictures to add further creations. For example you could turn it into a journal by writing about your day in the blank areas, play with some interesting fonts or add your favourite affirmations; build on what you find here. You are the artist so whatever you create will be perfect!

Happy colouring!

Wishing you many continued blessings,

Tammy

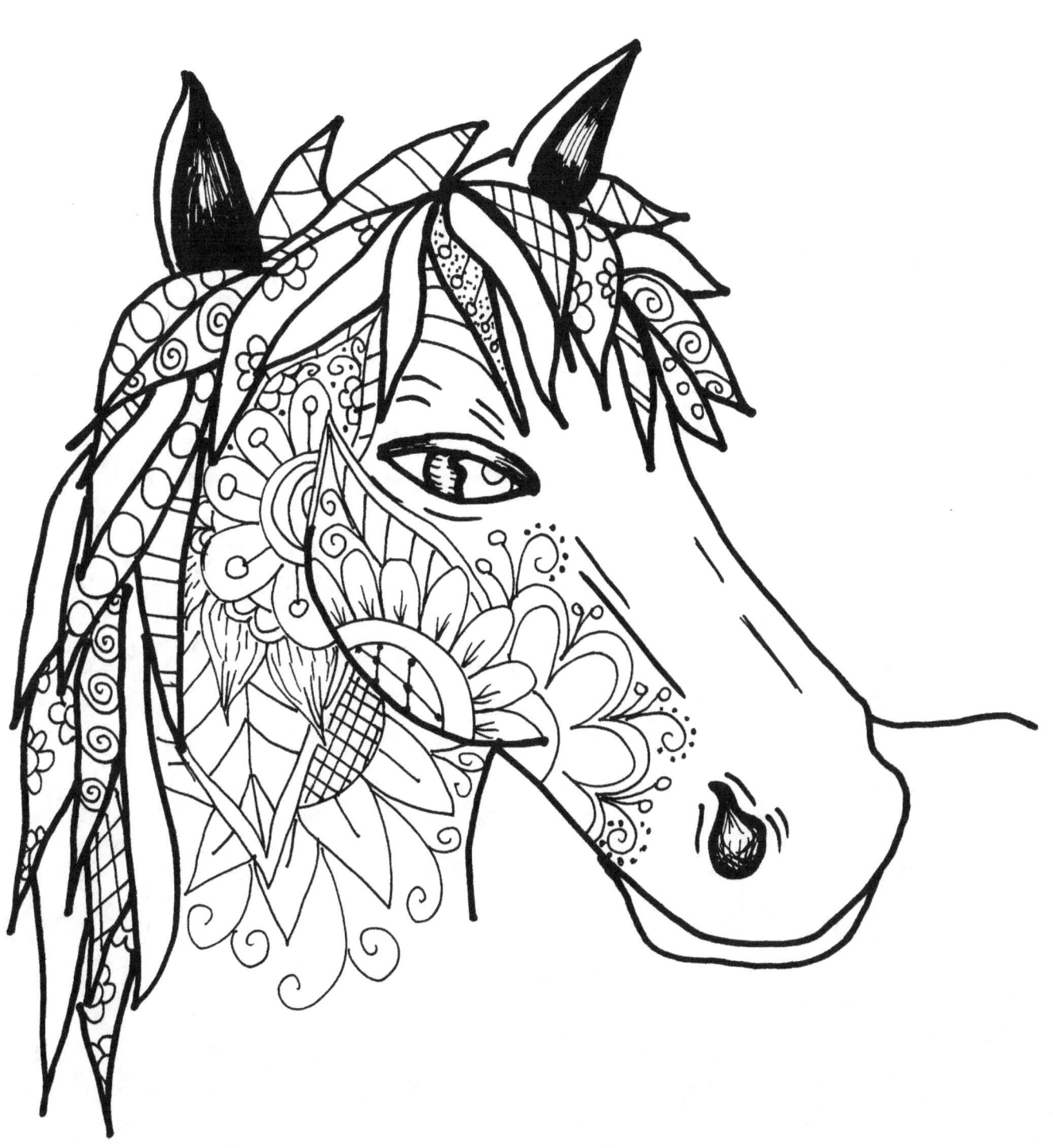

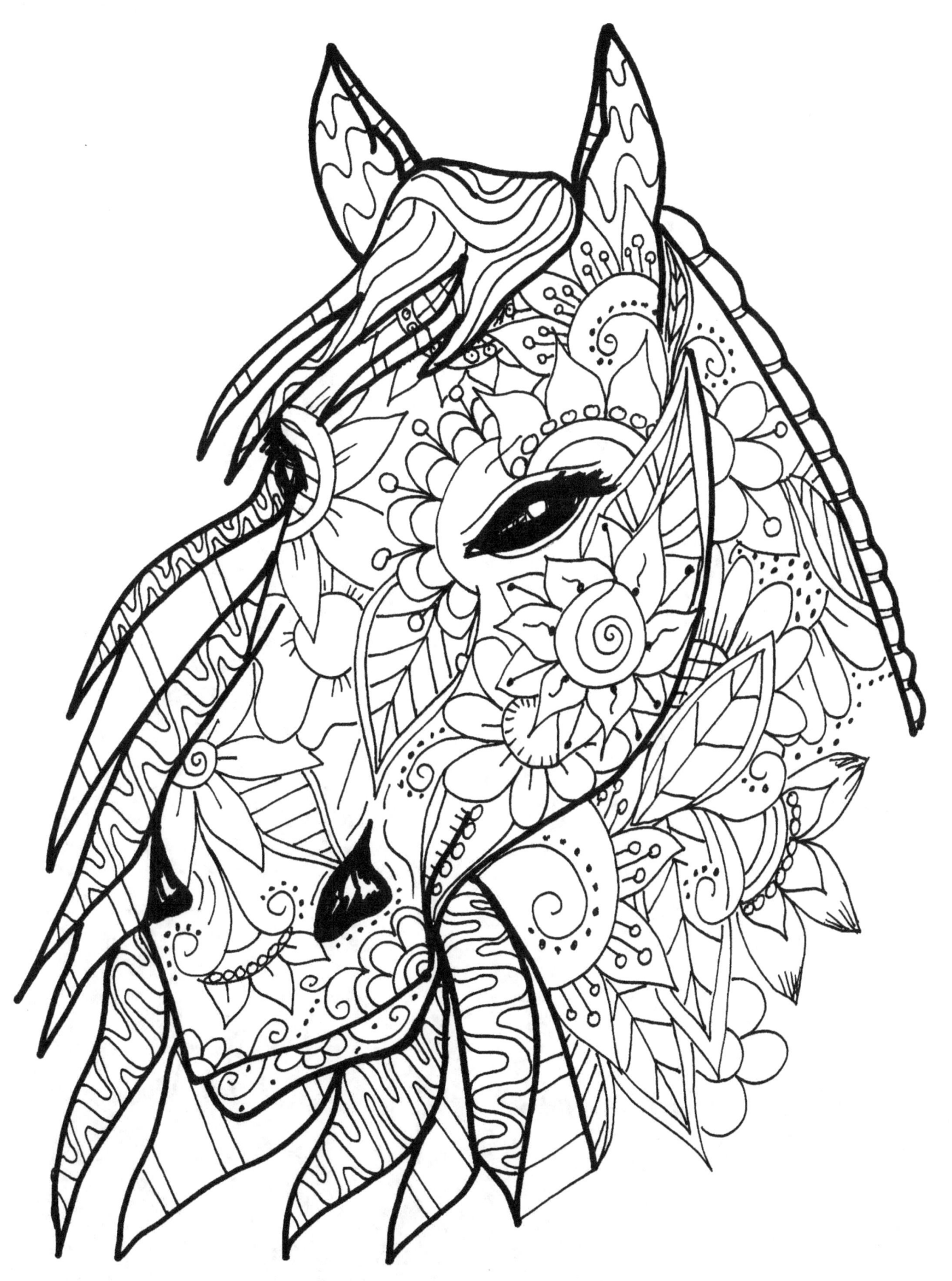

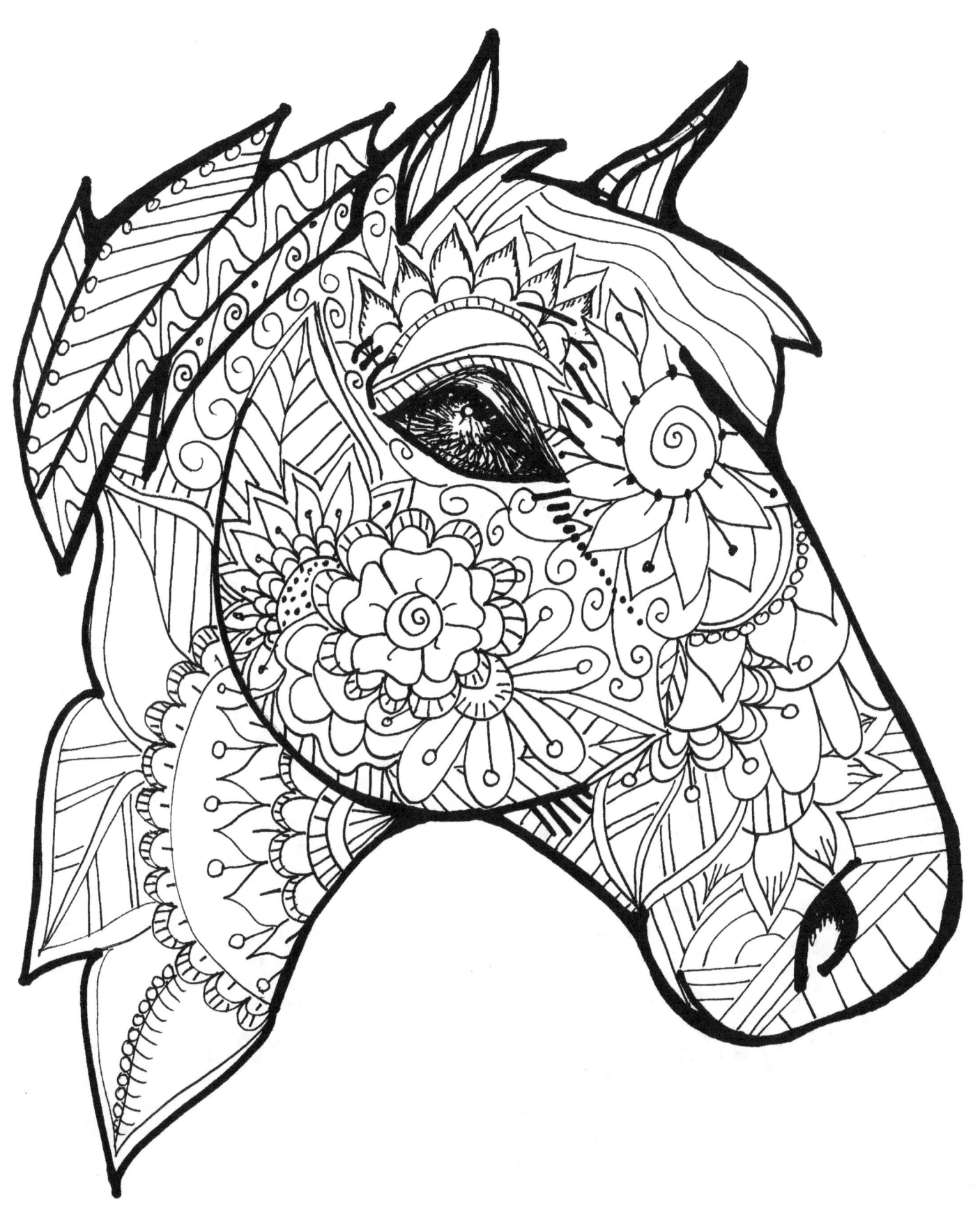

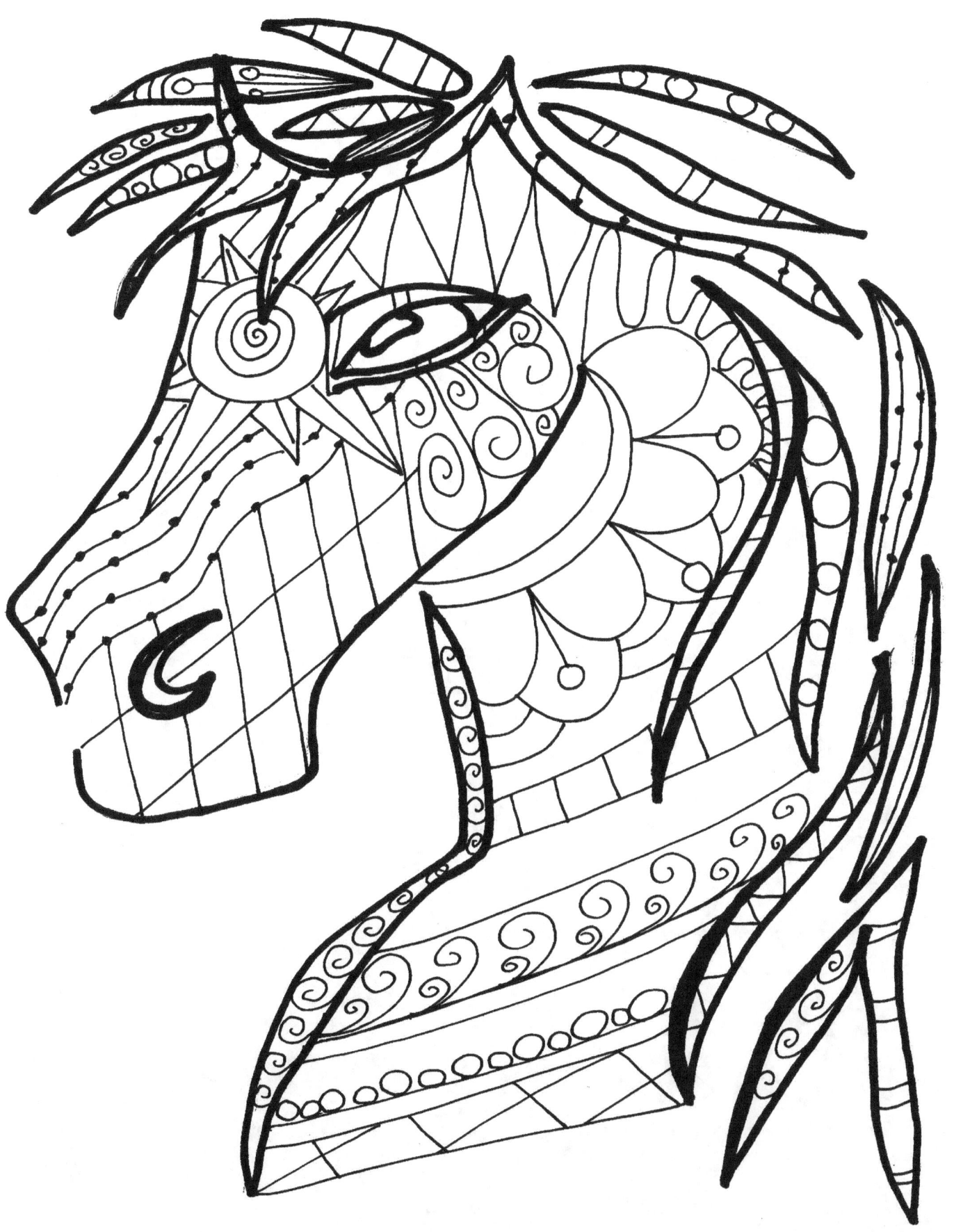

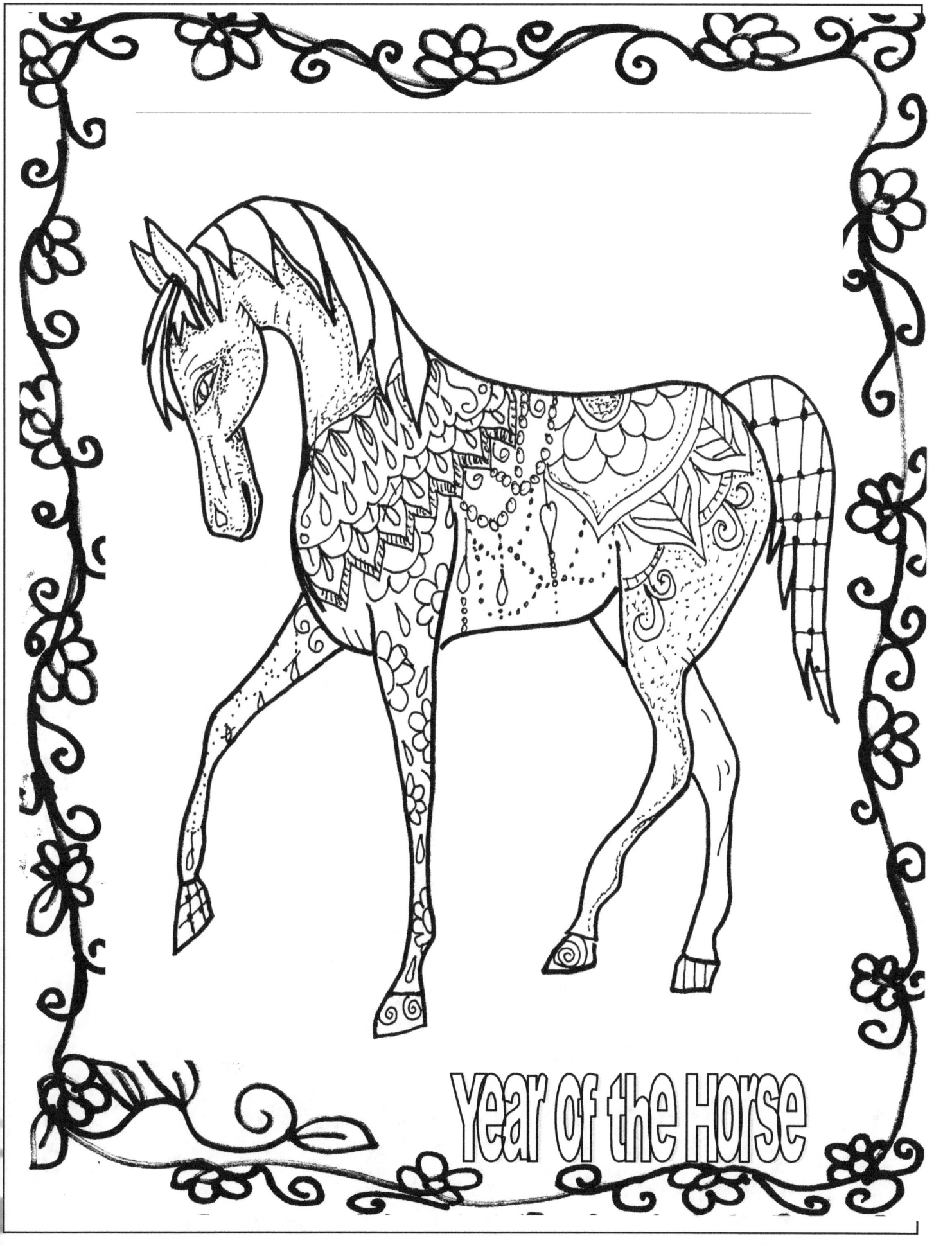

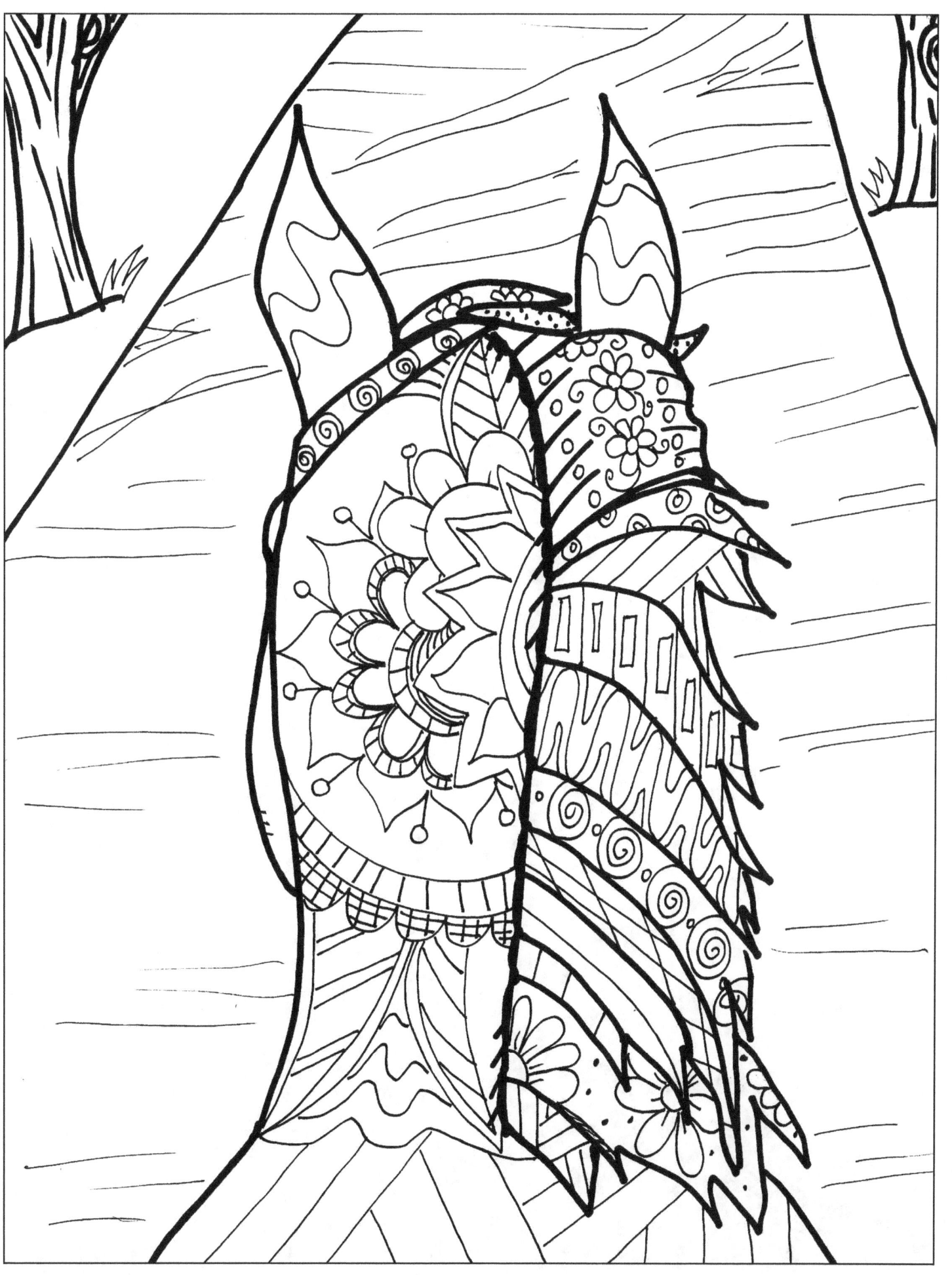

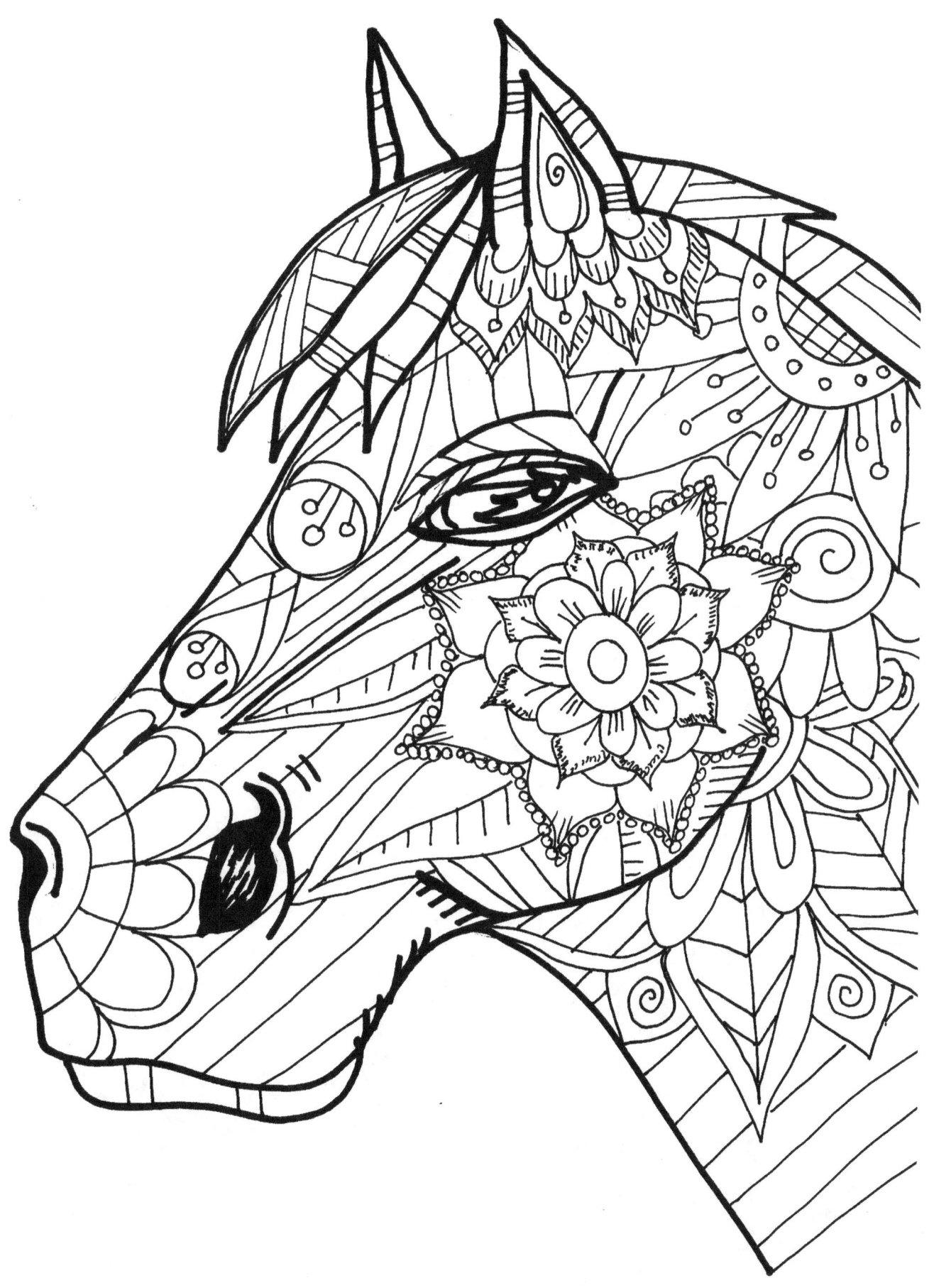

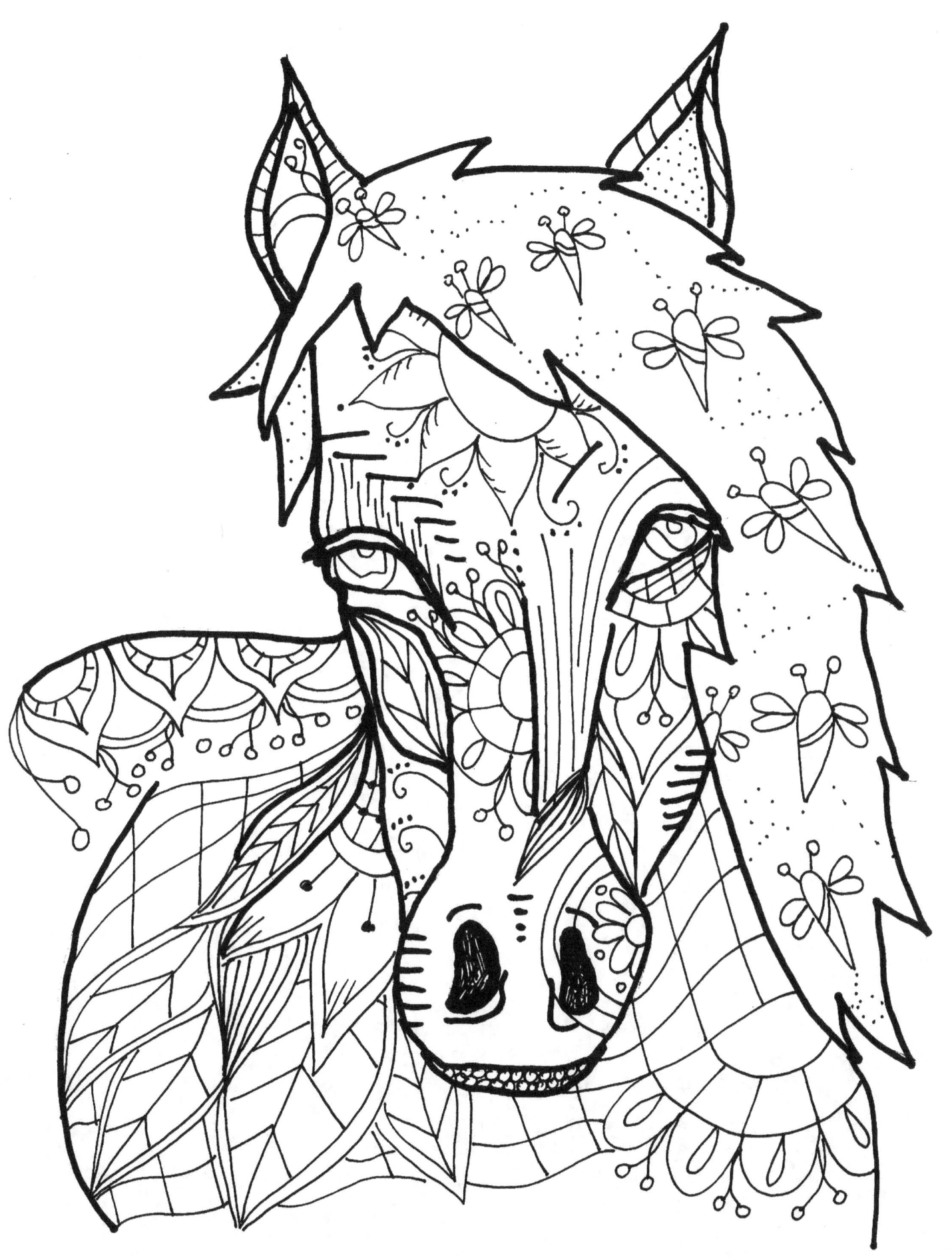

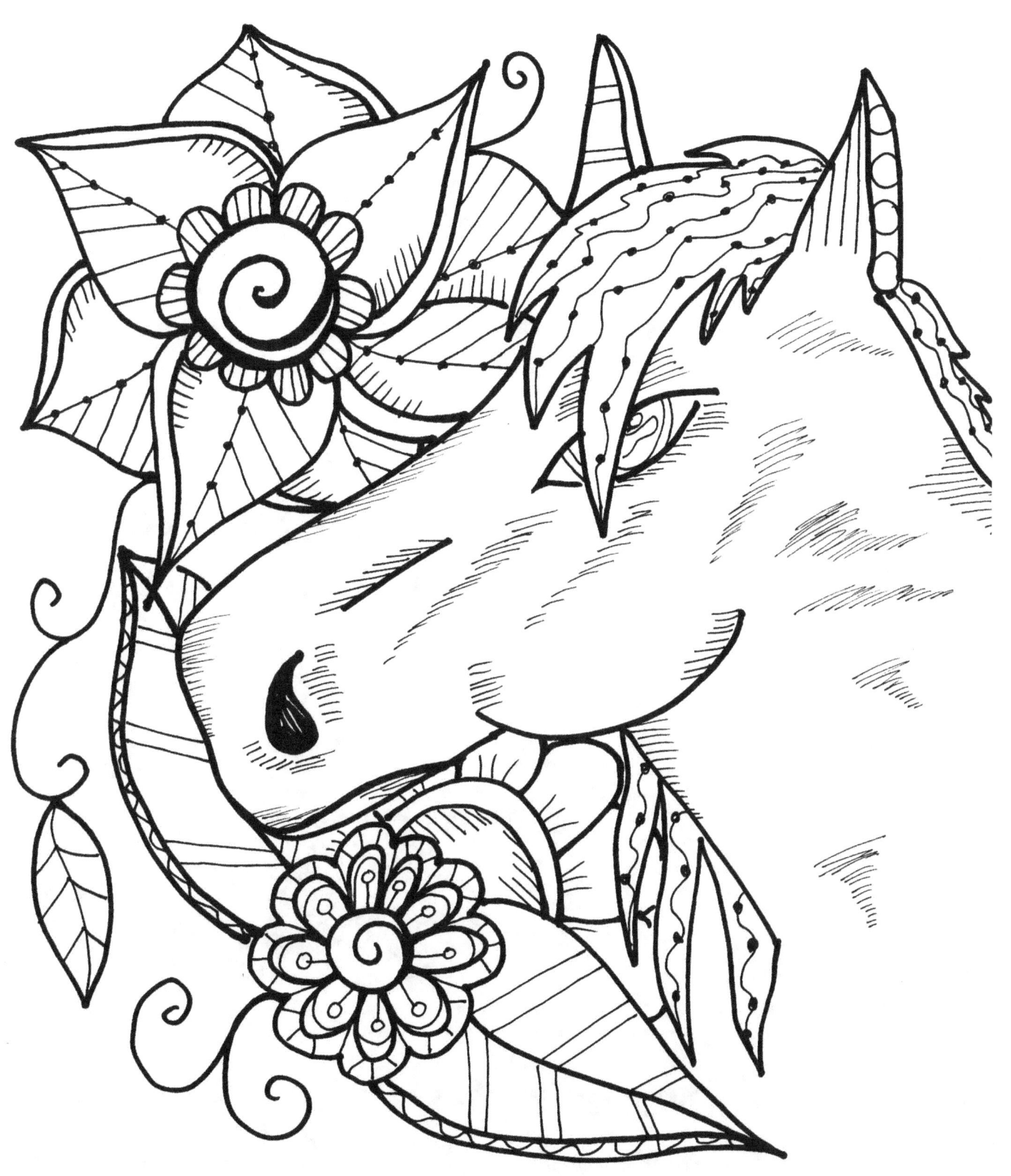

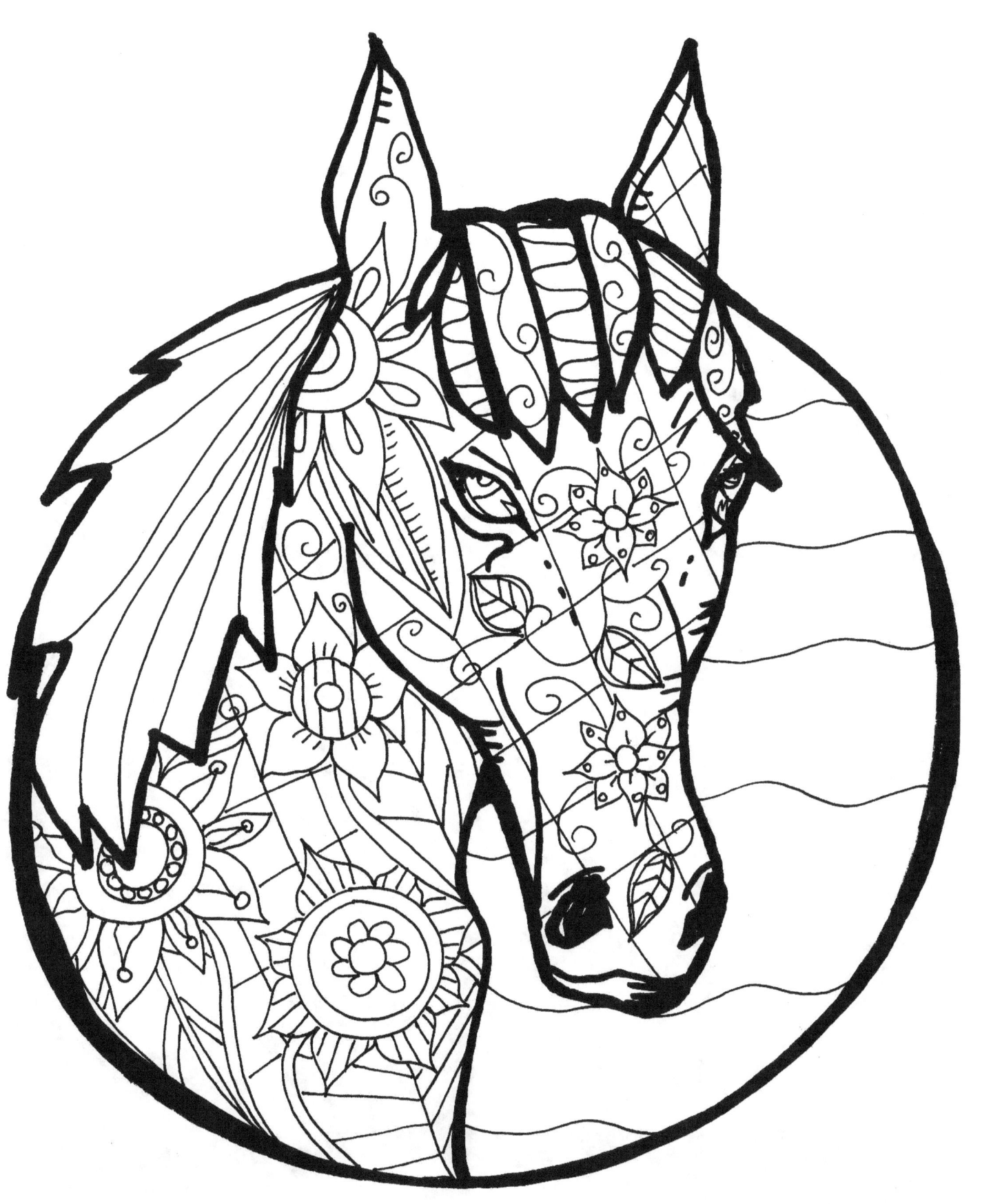

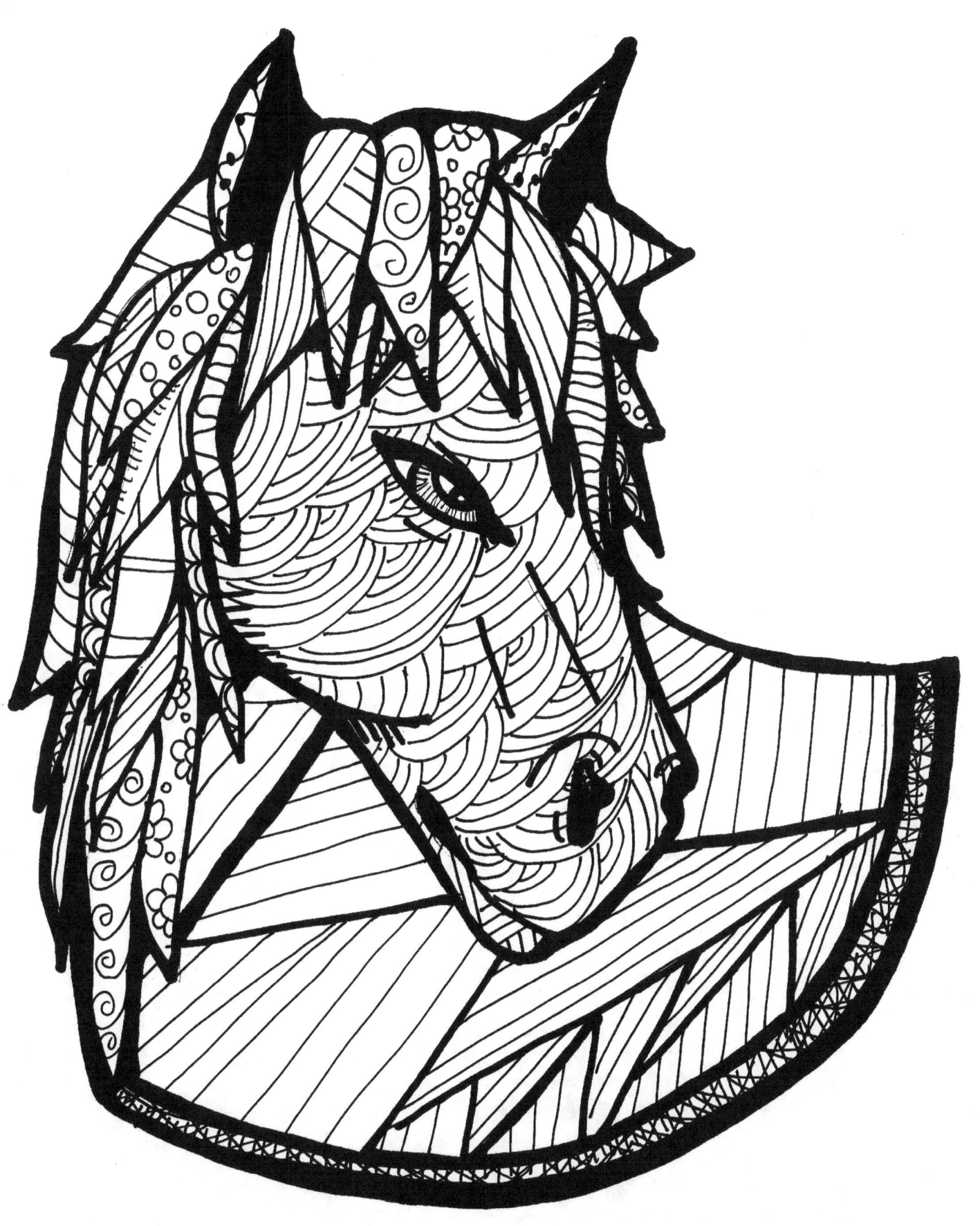

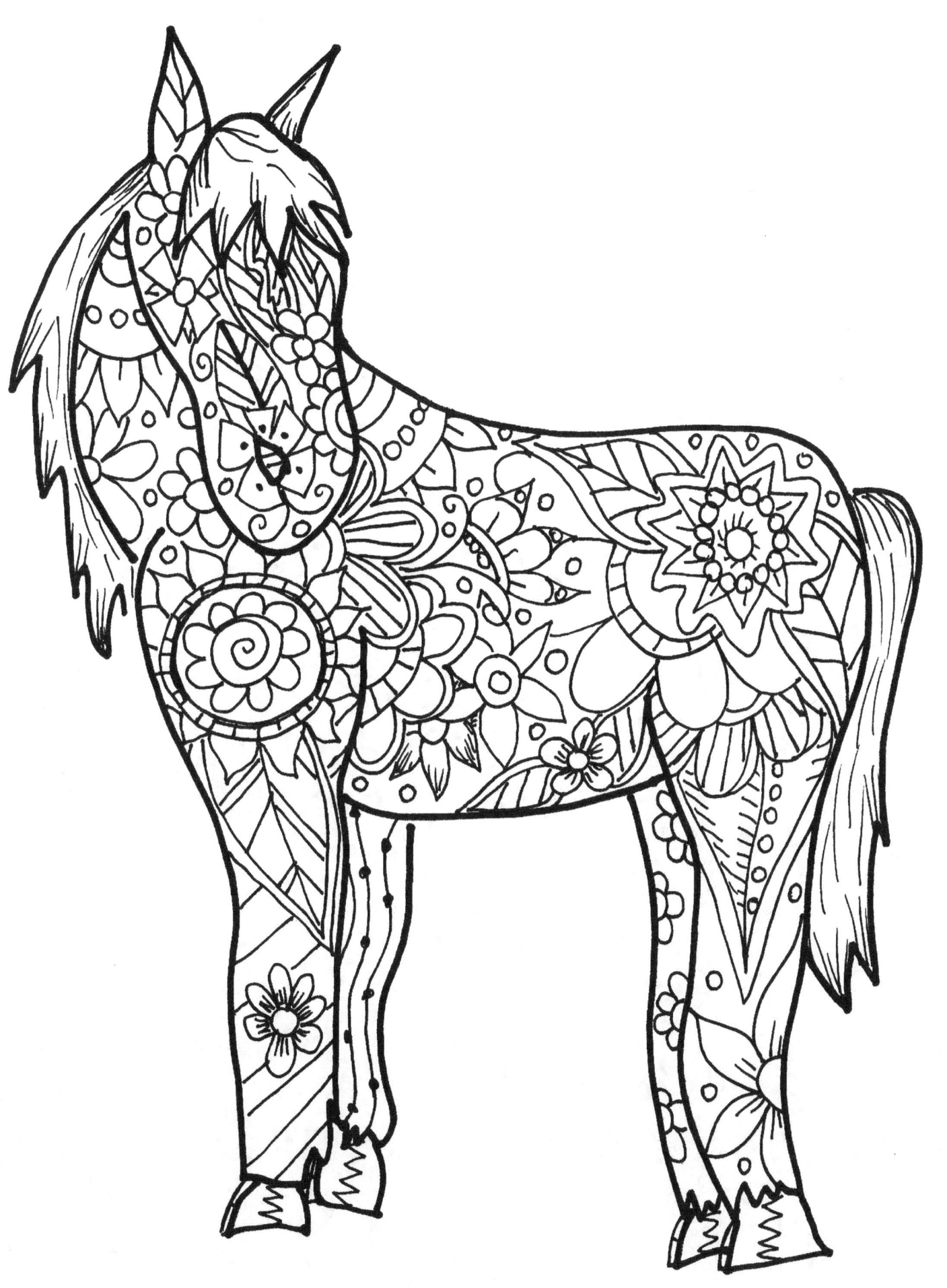

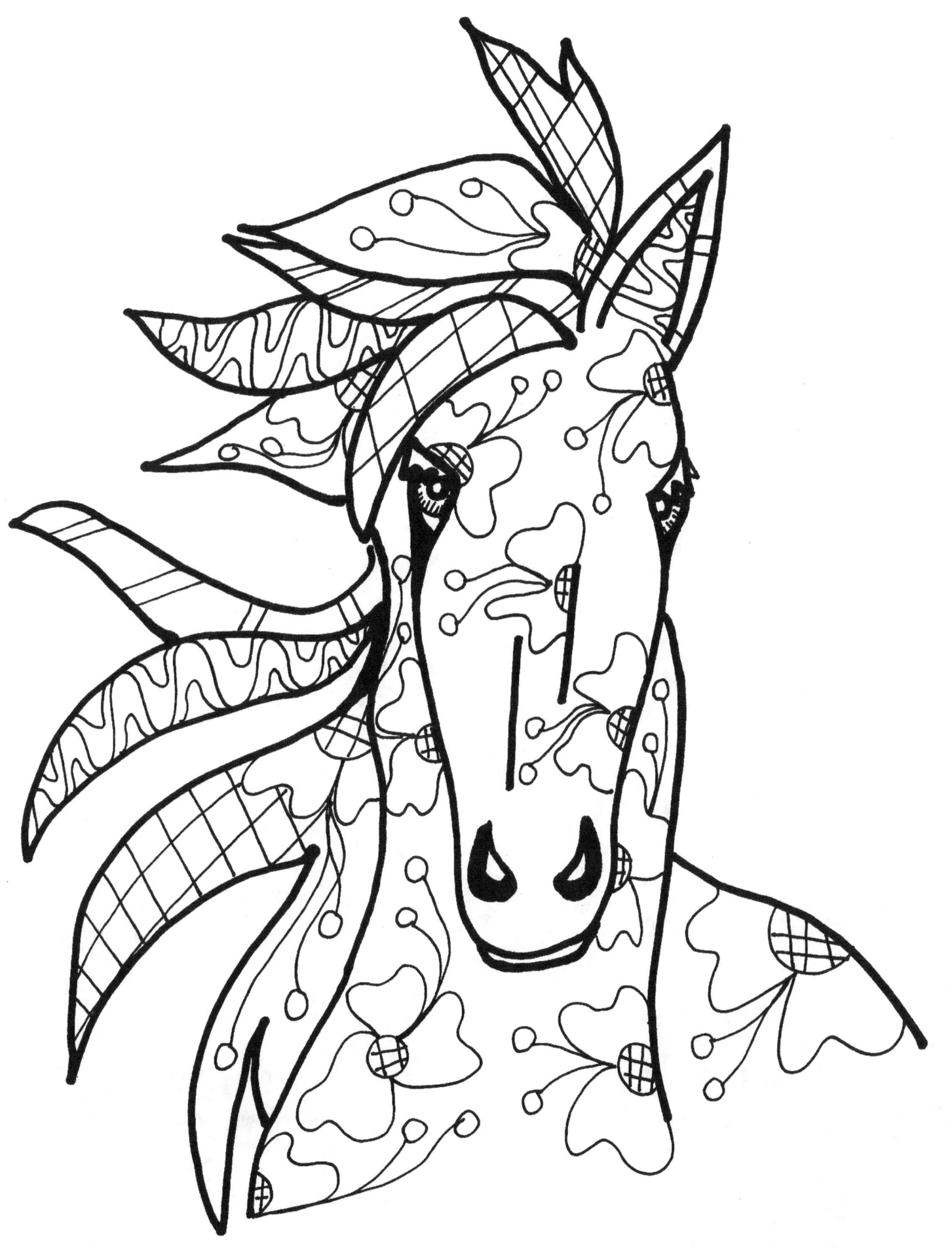

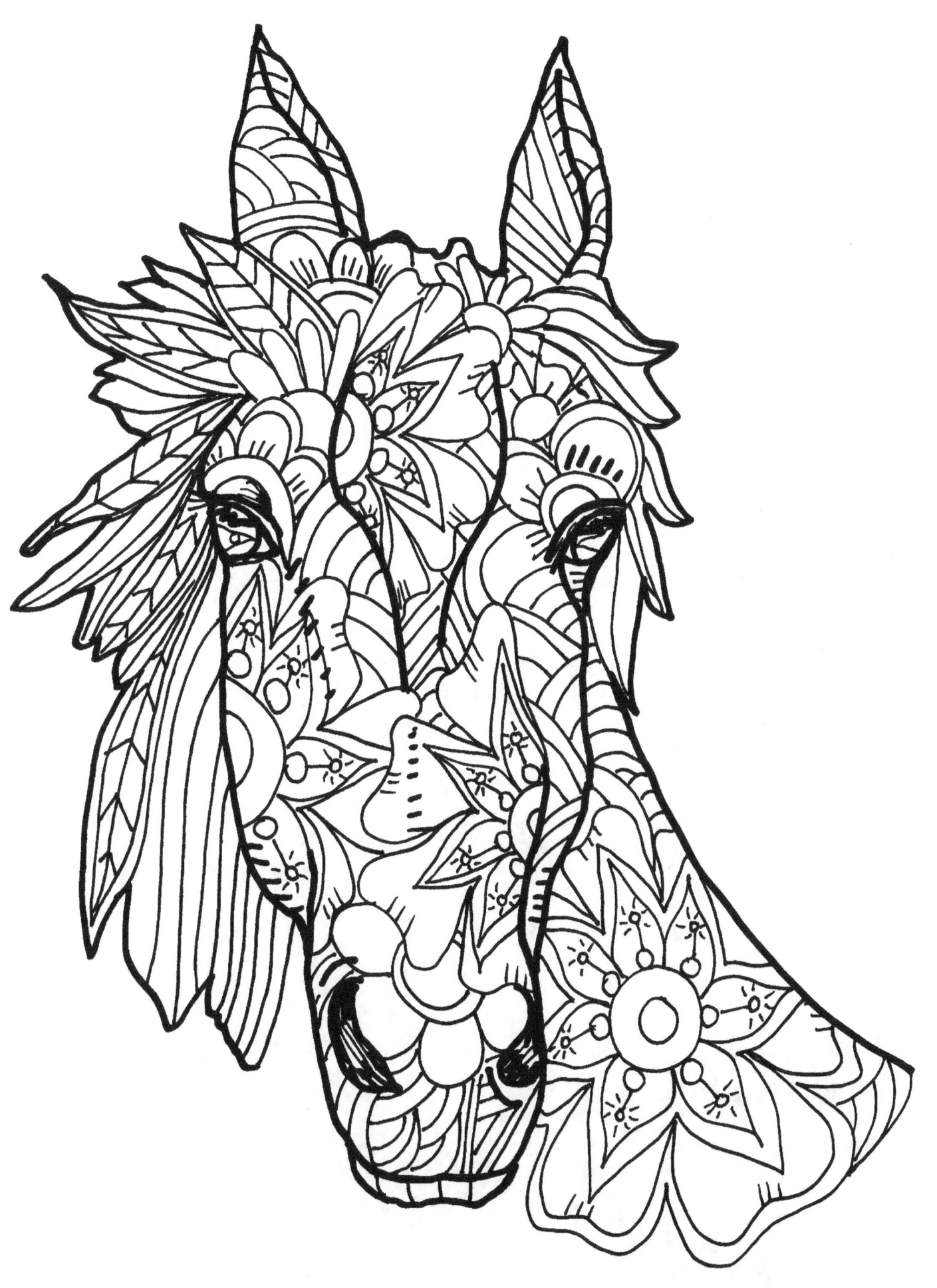

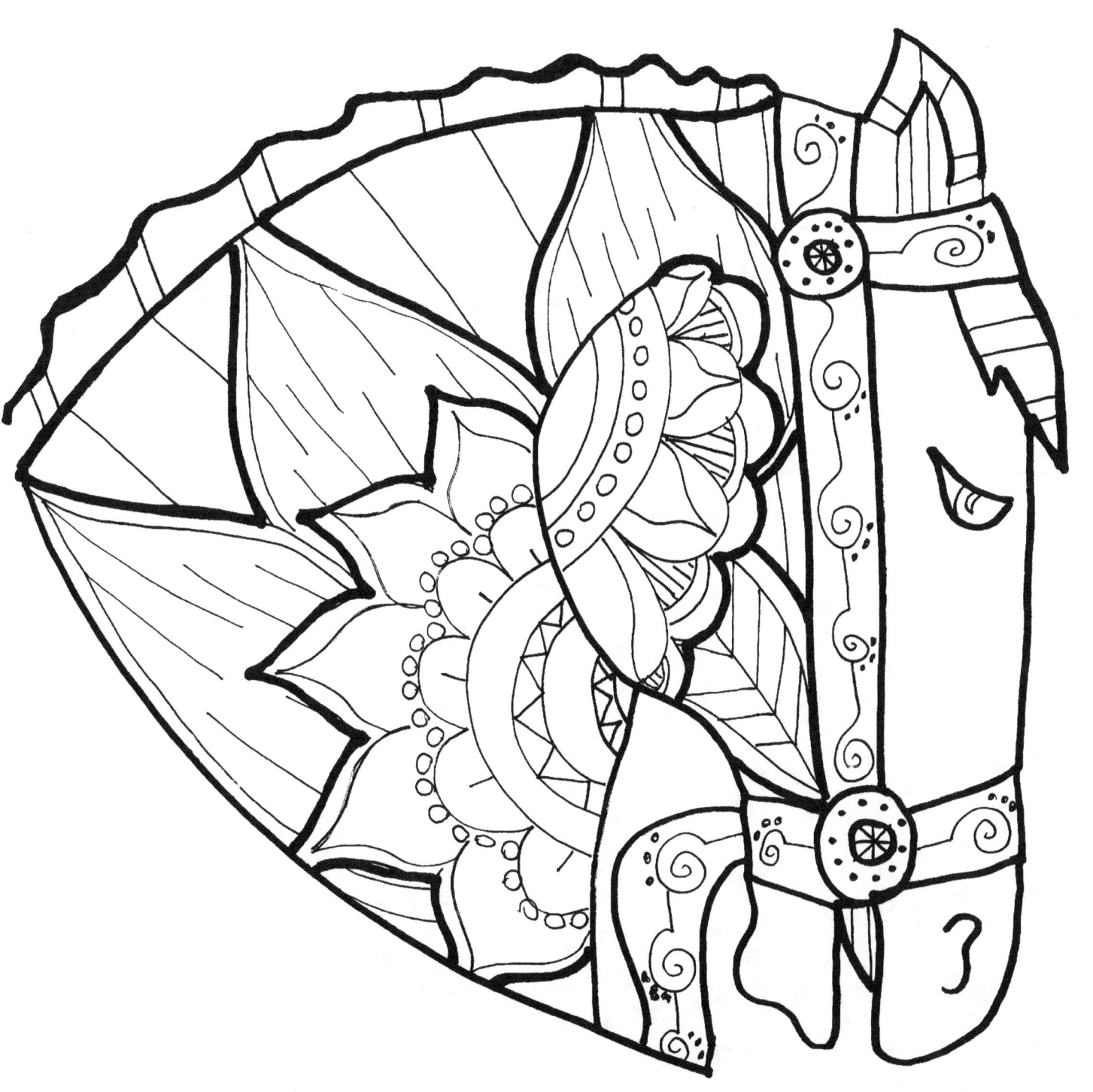

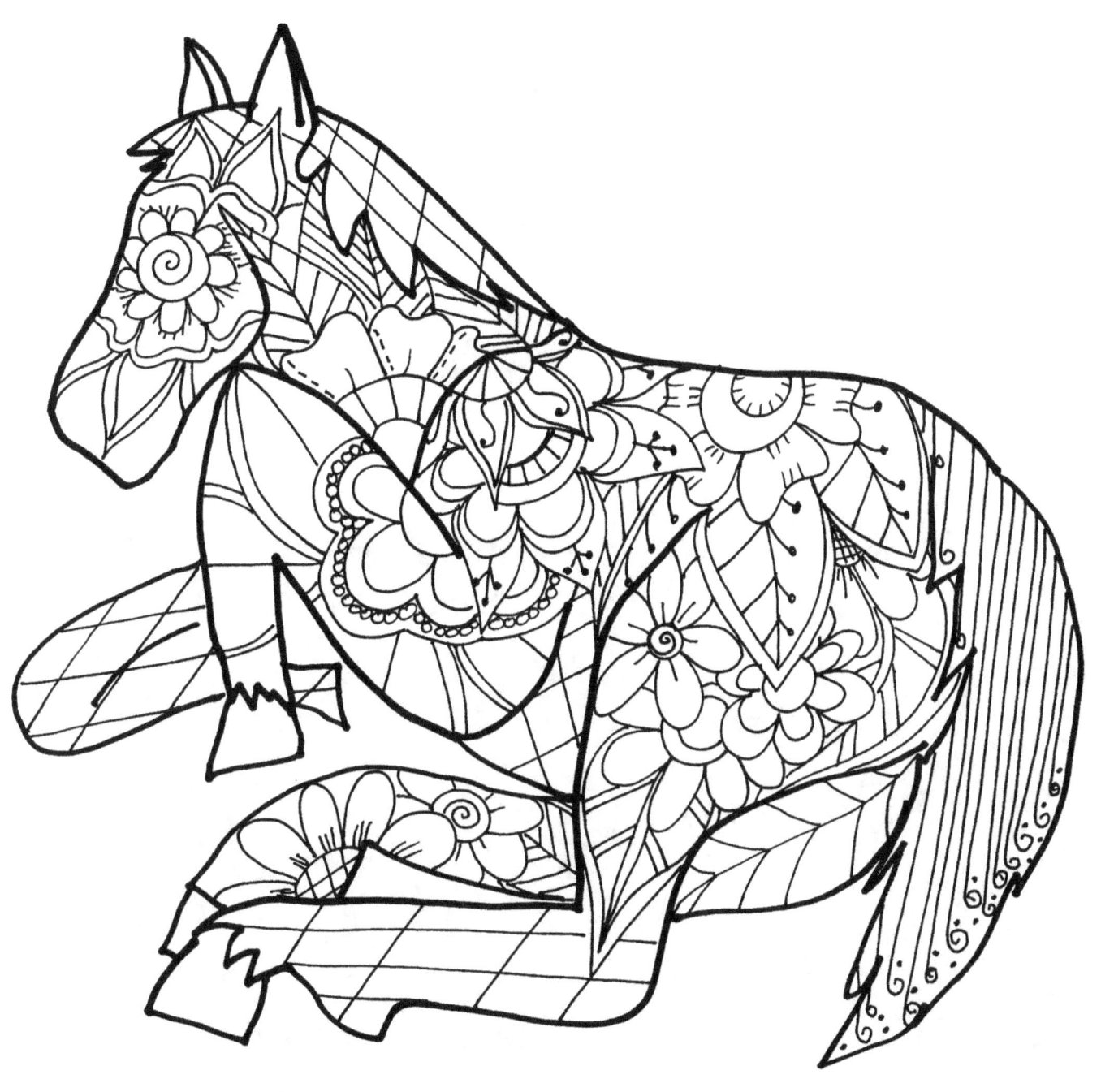

Everyday a blessing

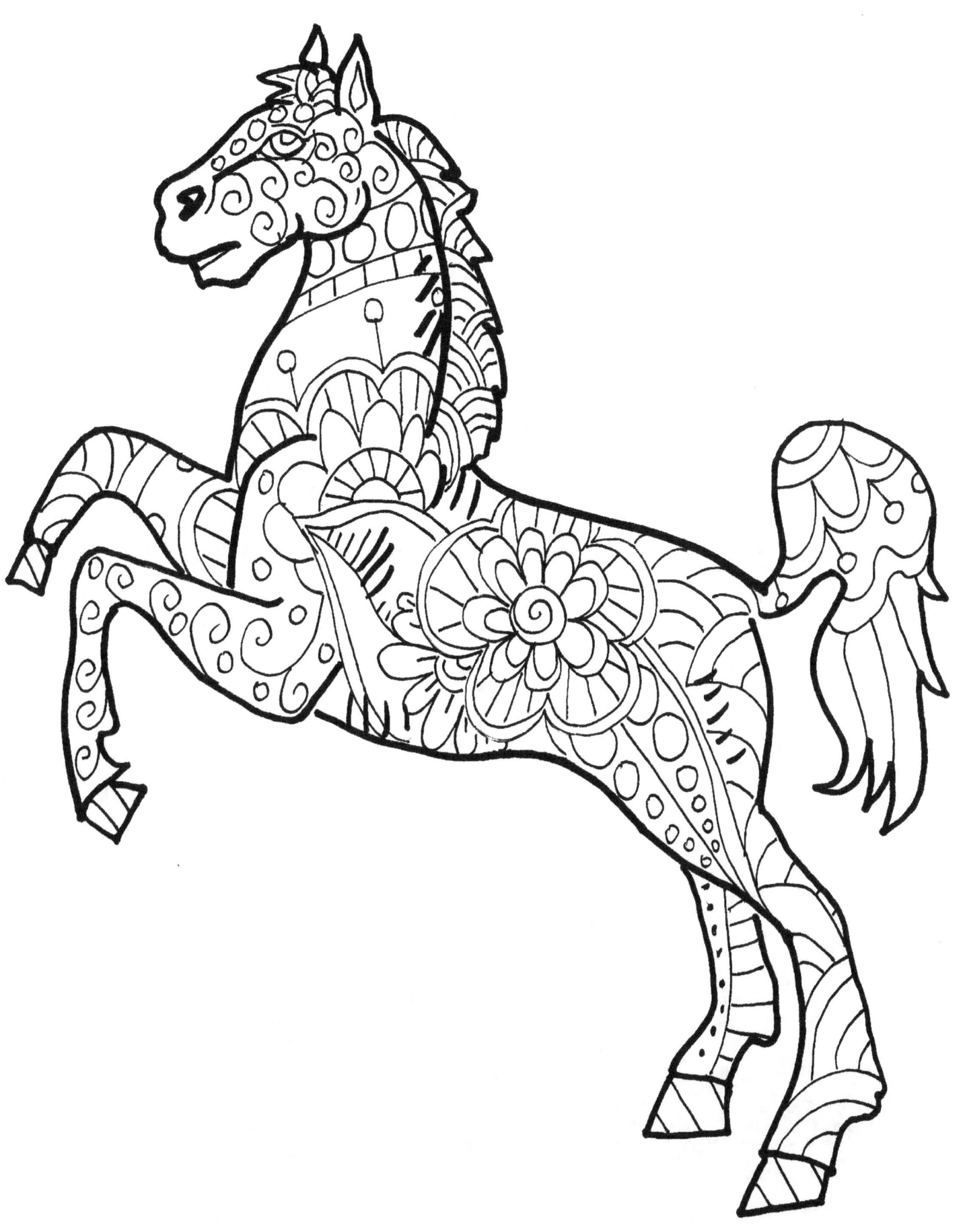

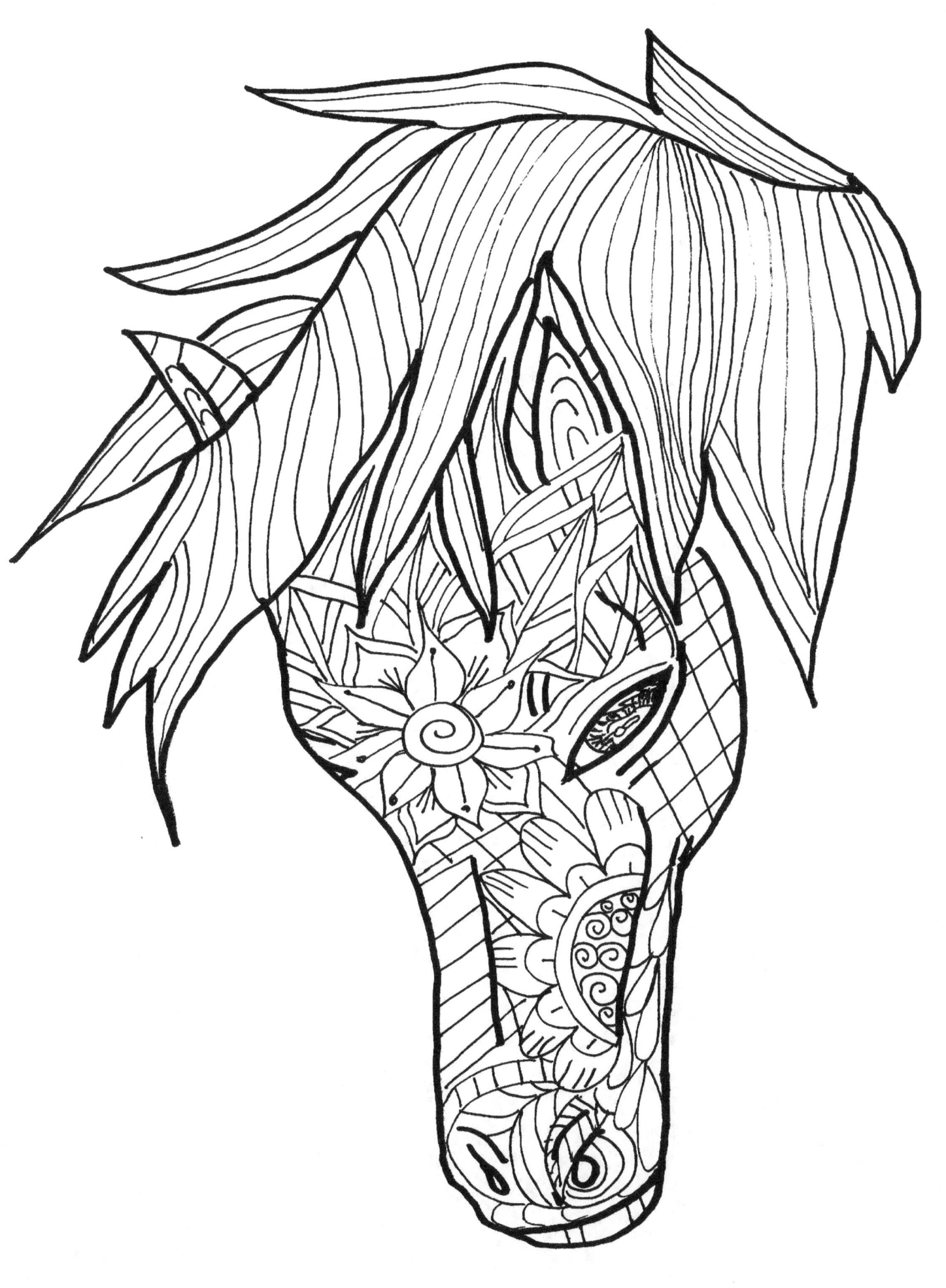

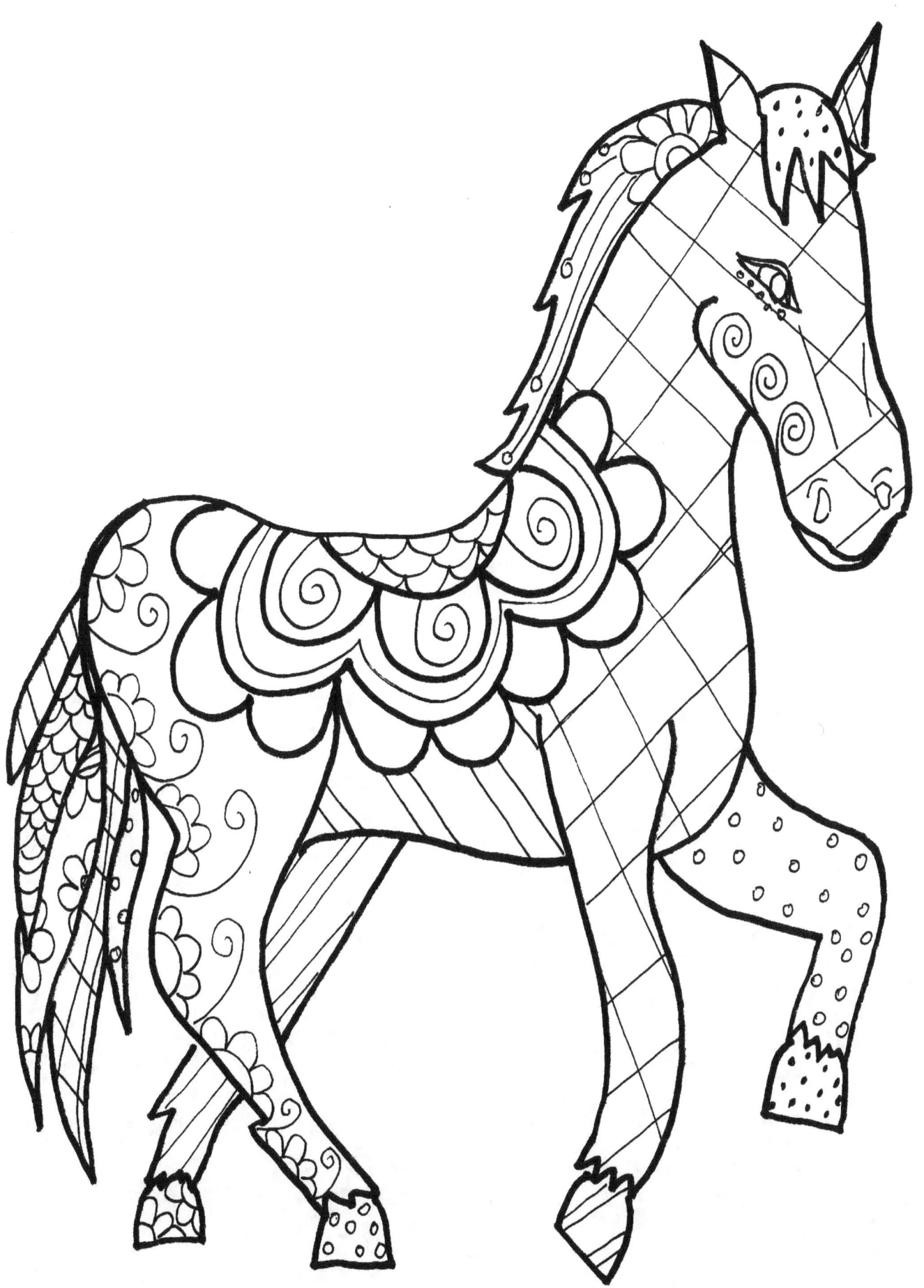

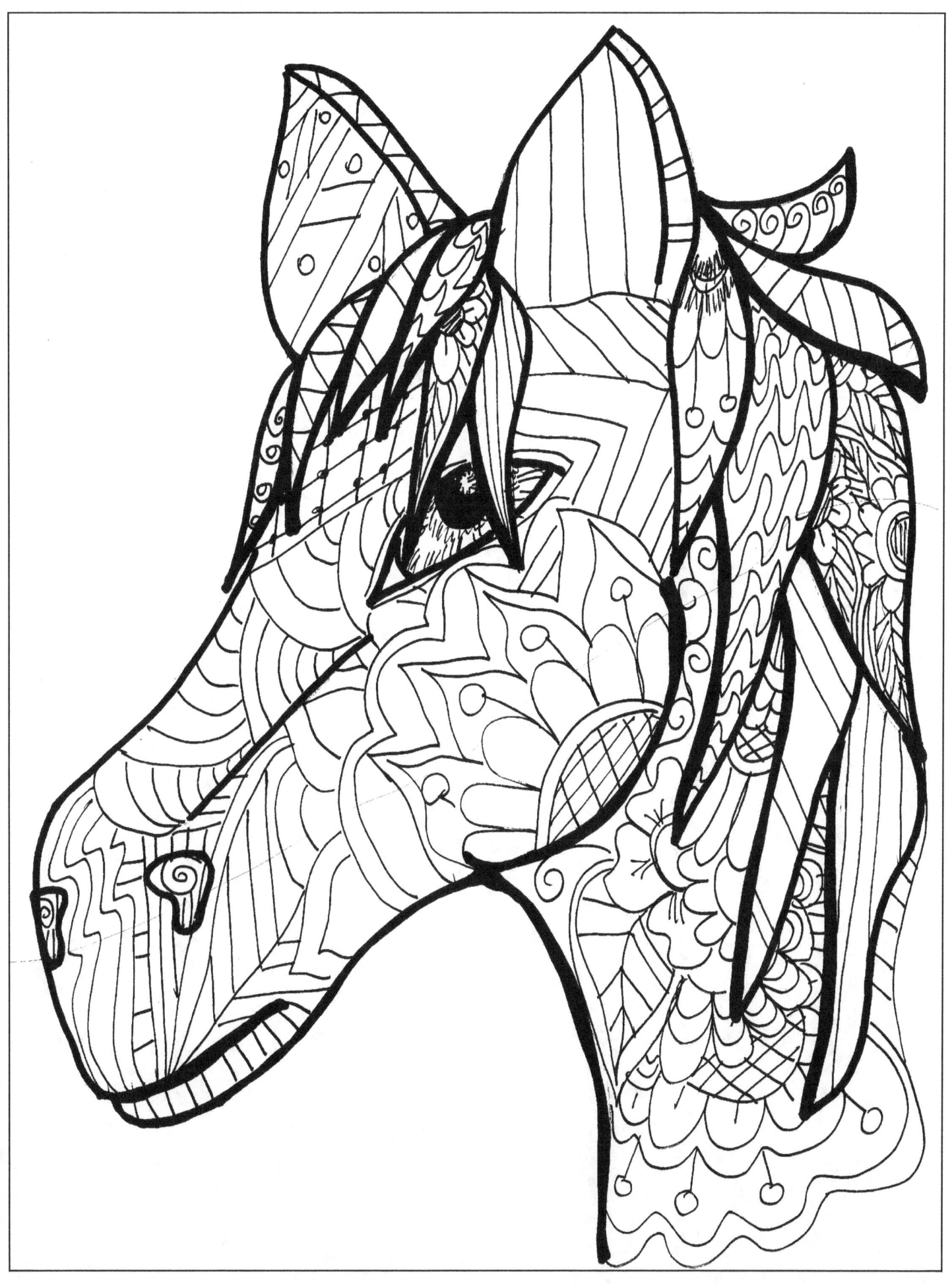

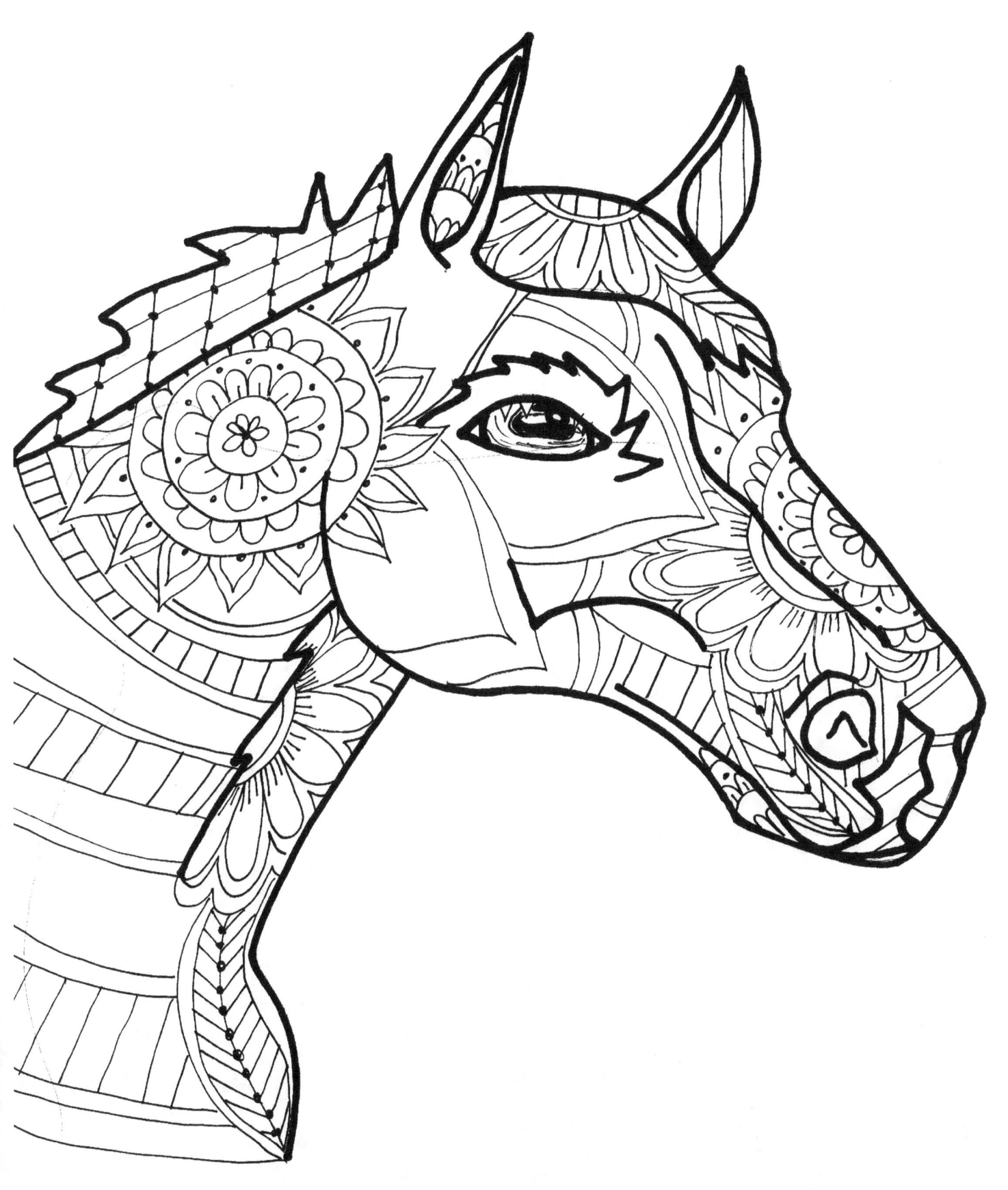

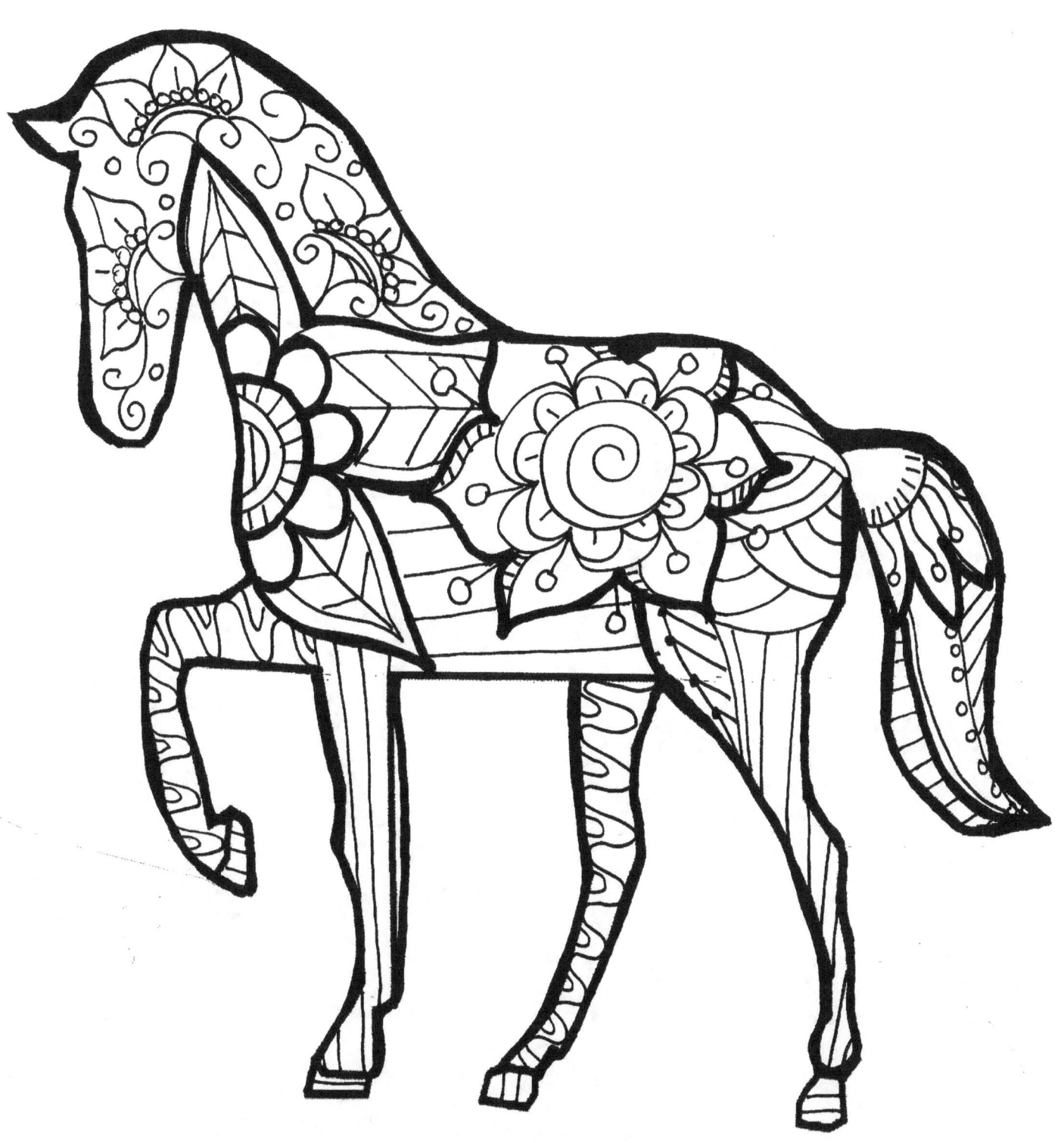

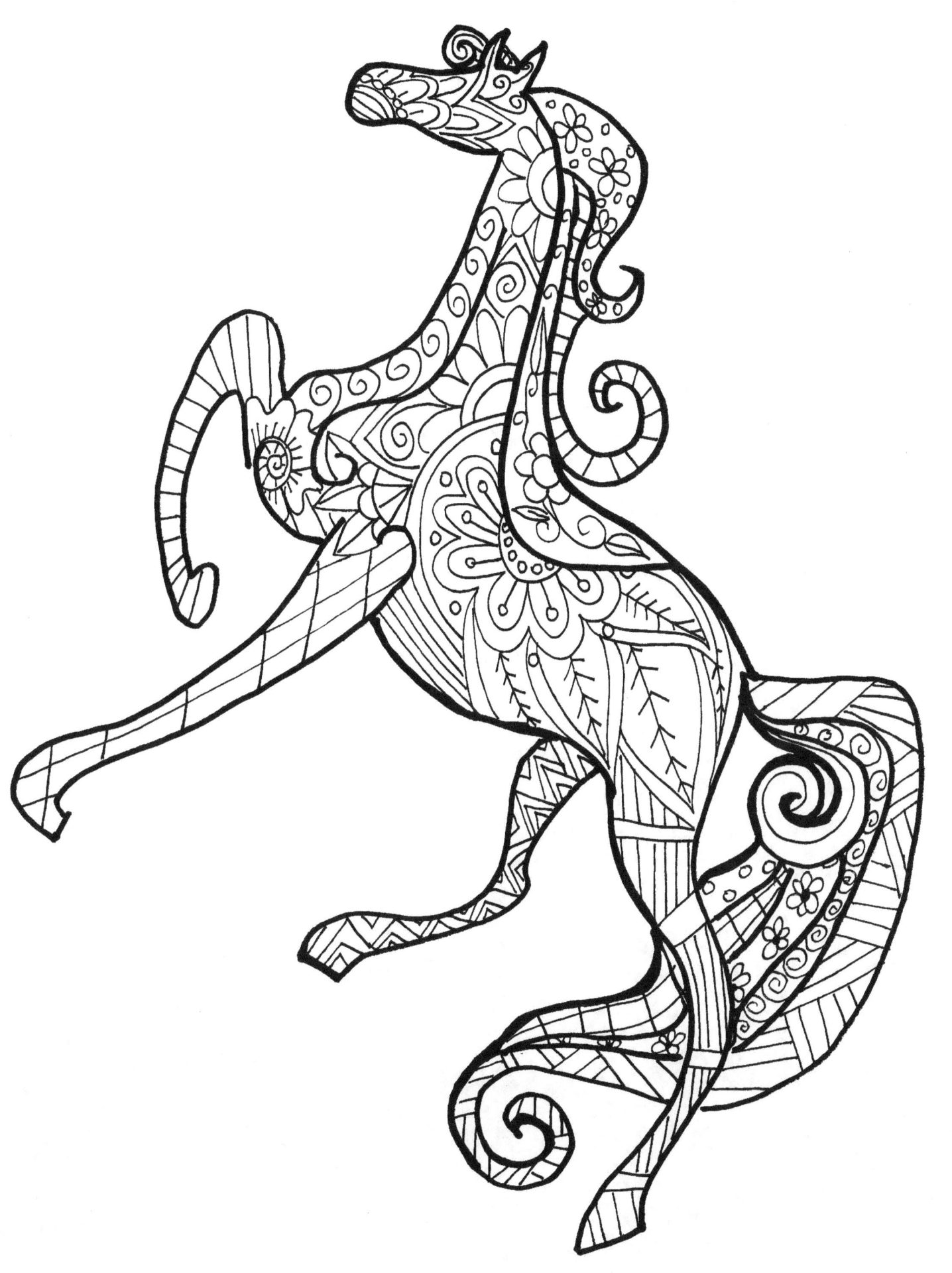

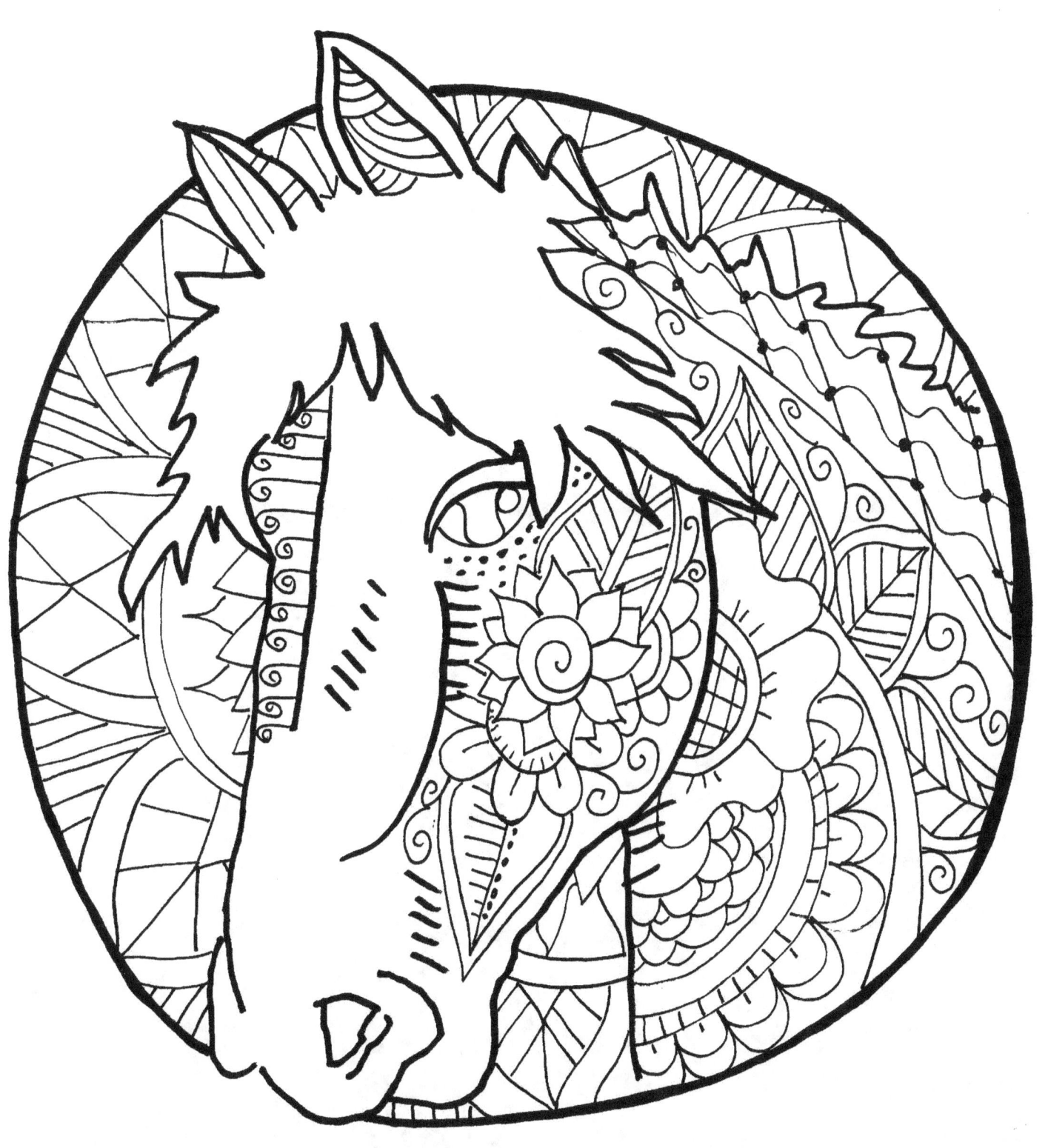

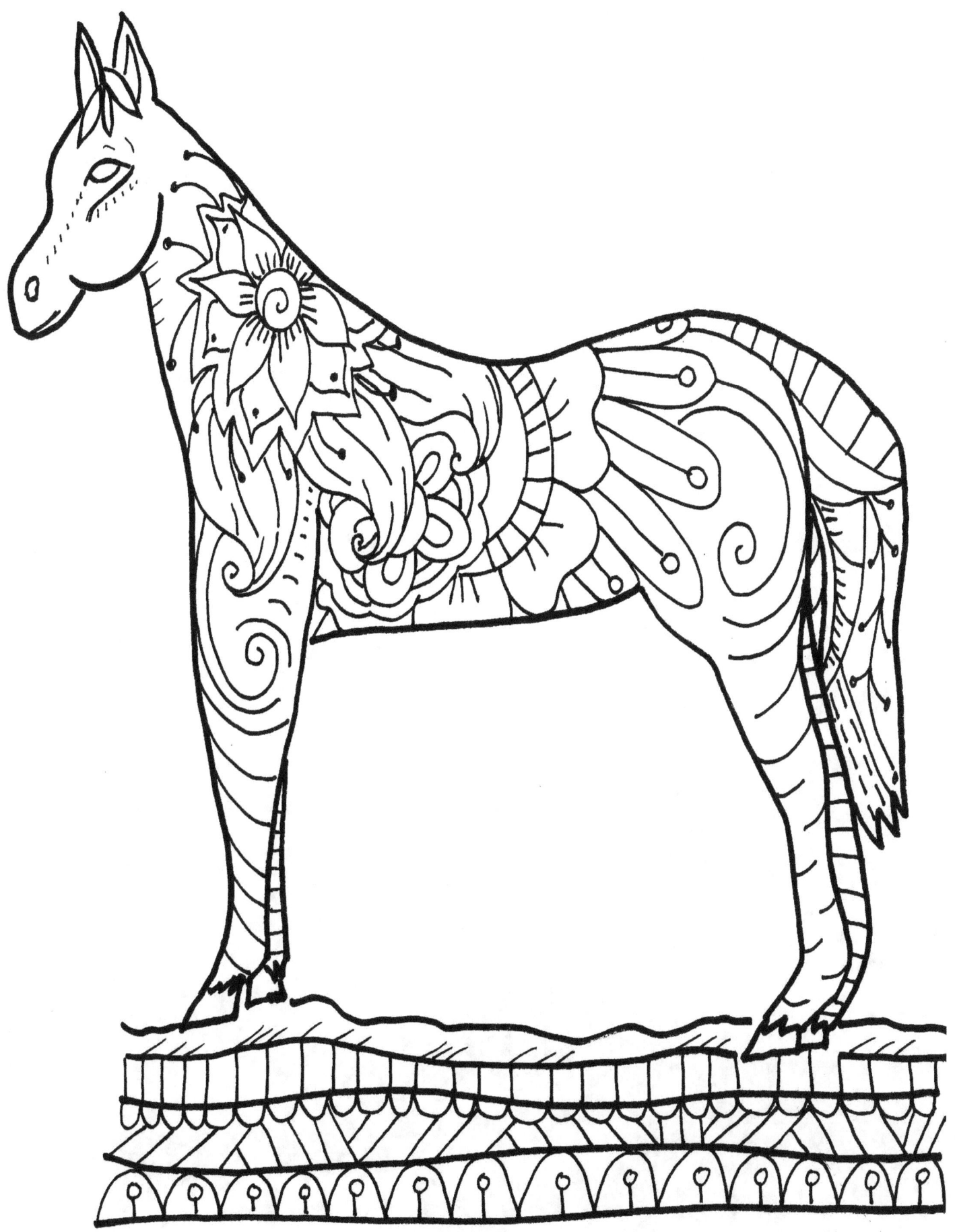

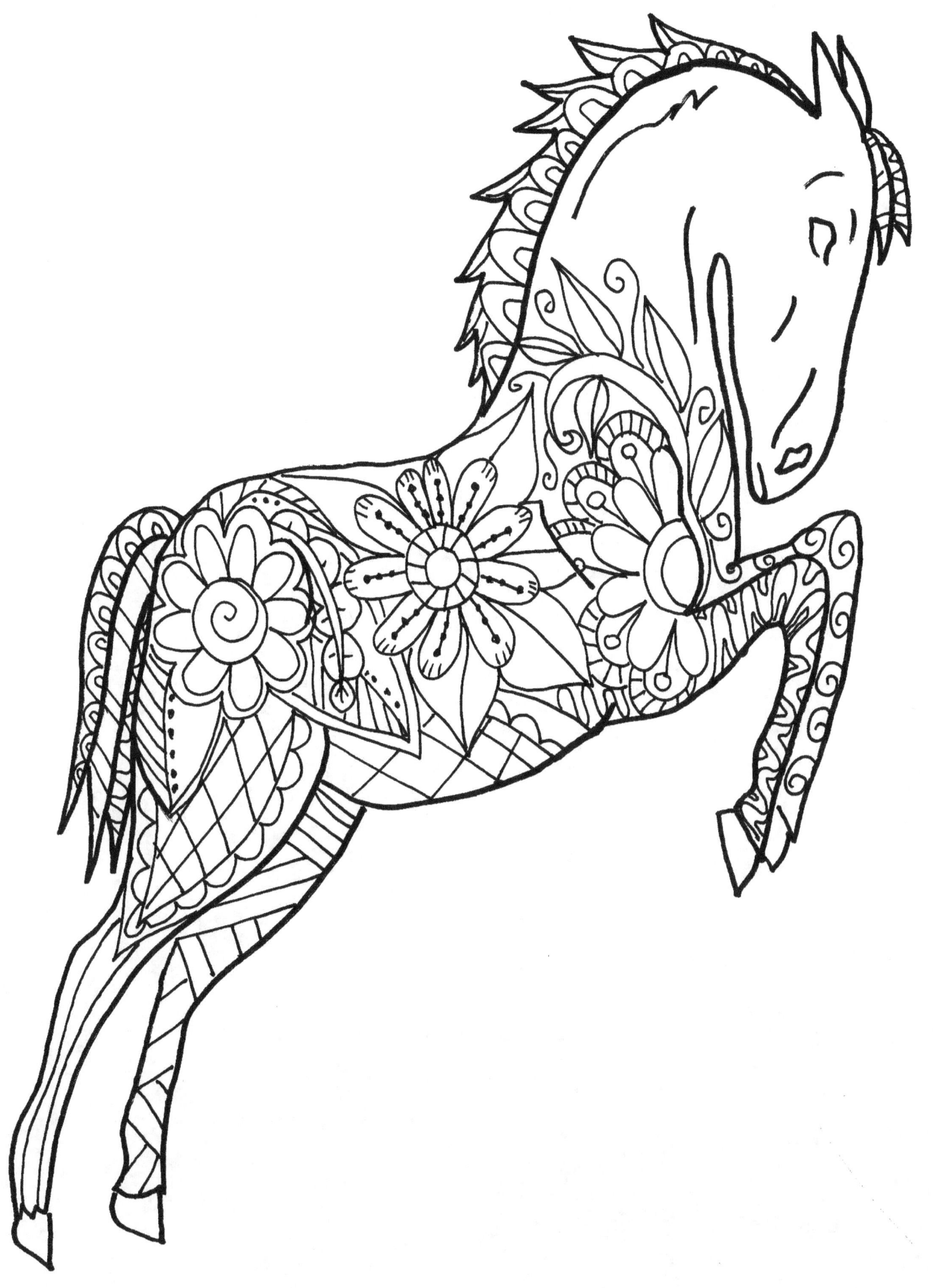

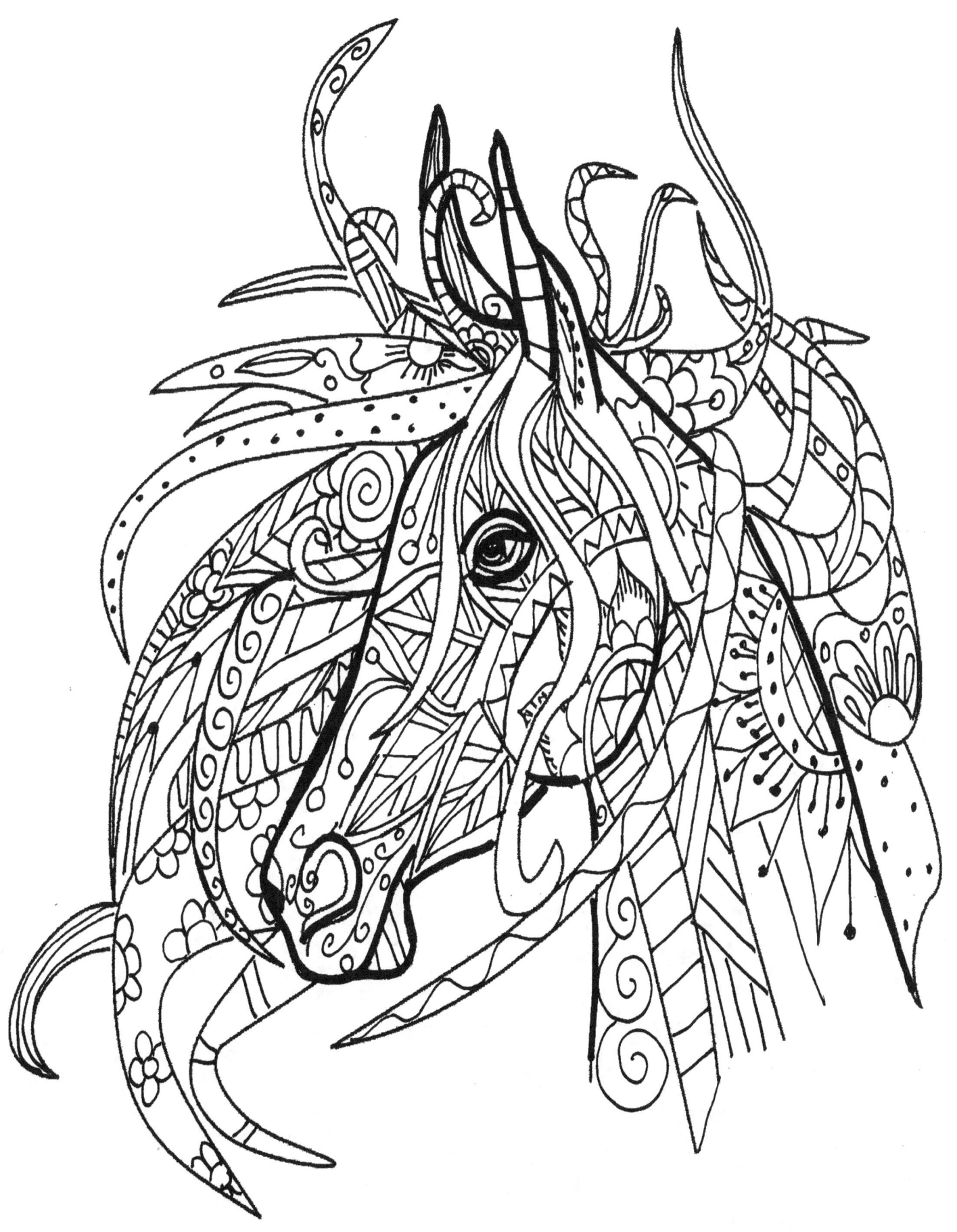

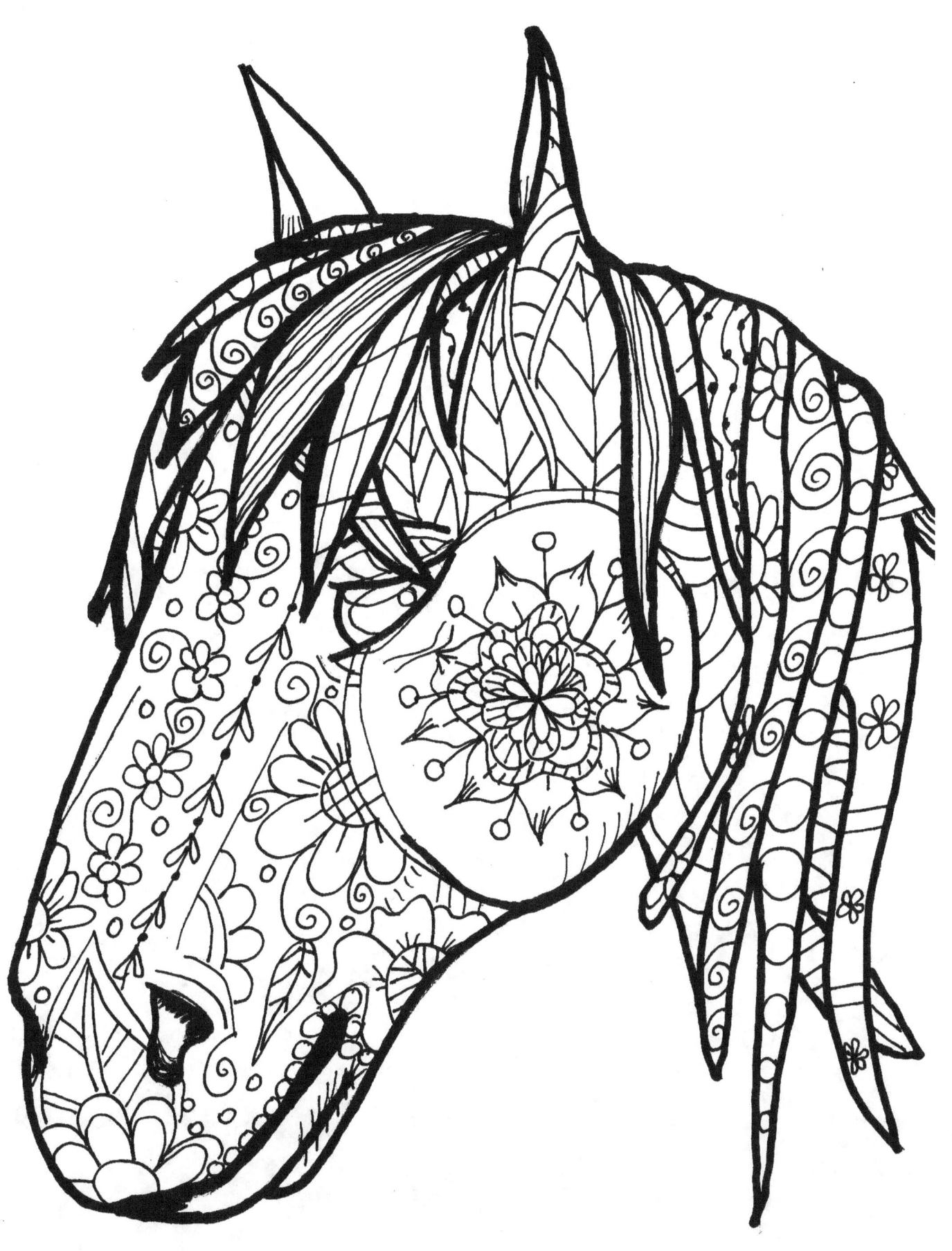

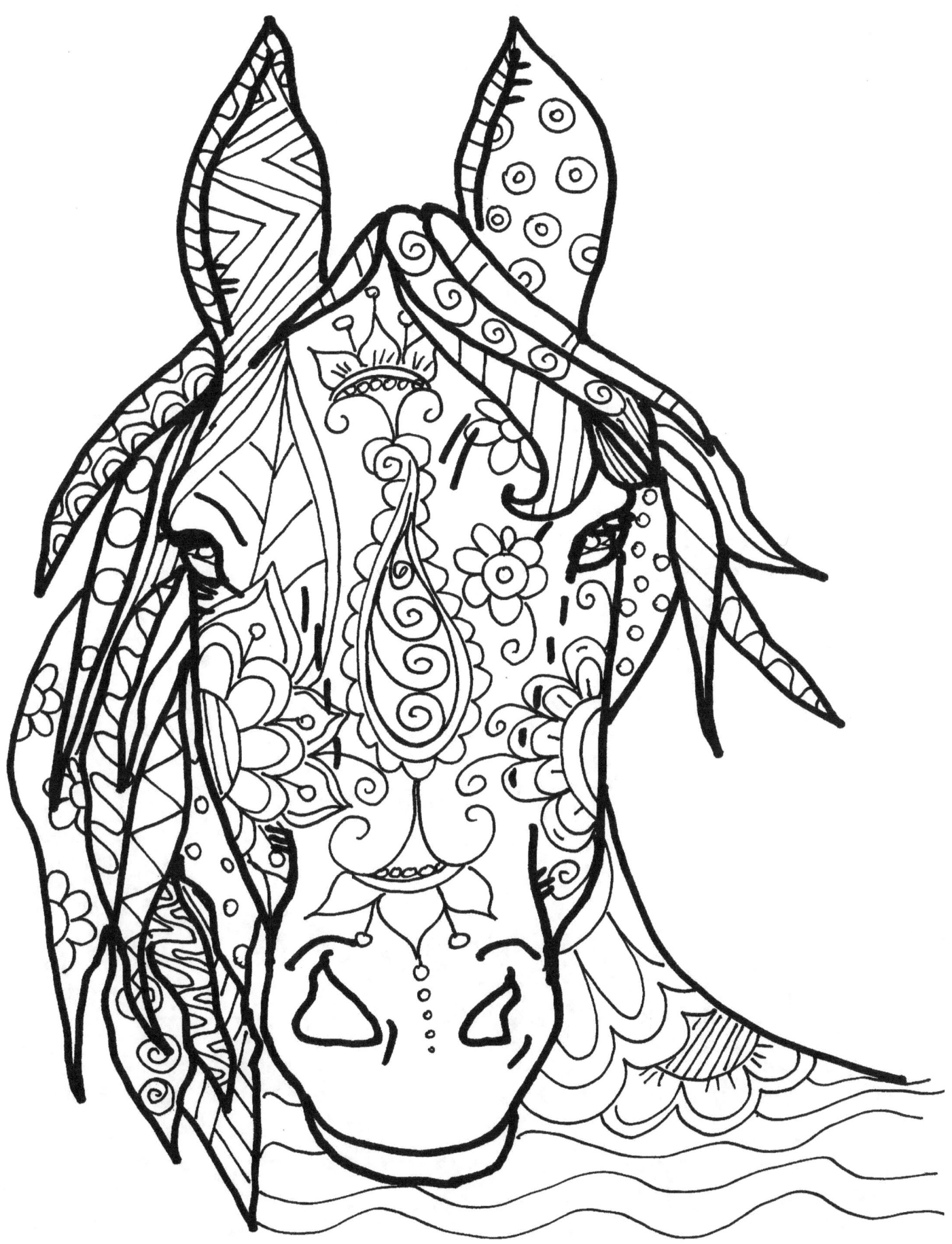

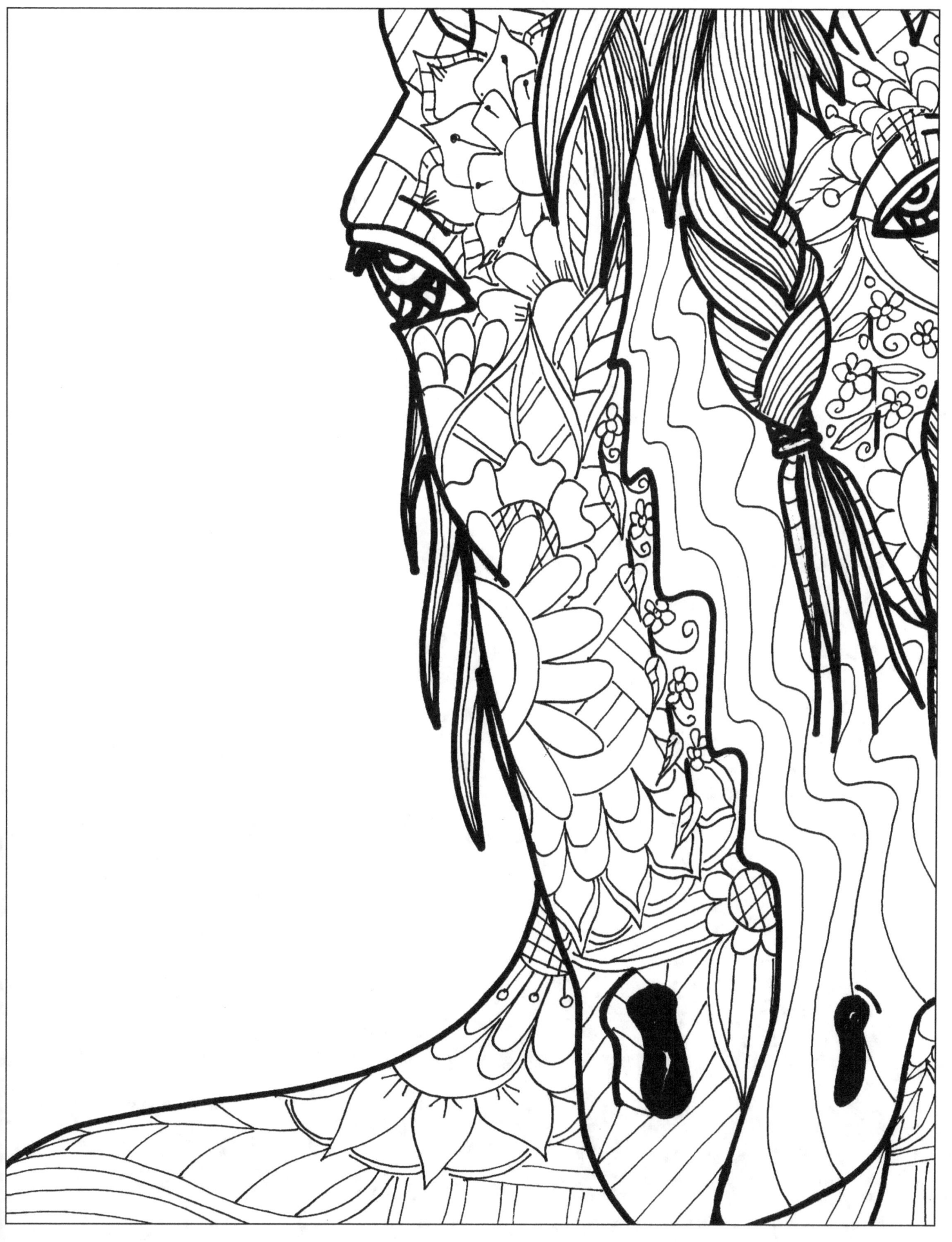

Year of the Horse

People born in the year of the Horse are said to be flexible and loyal friends. They are easy going, independent and usually have a positive attitude. Horses could work on being less stubborn and more persistent.

The Elements

Wood Horse: Good leader, decision maker, imaginative, opinionated

Fire Horse: Intelligent, passionate, very energetic and sensitive

Earth Horse: Optimistic, grounded, practical

Metal Horse: Active, enjoys challenge, stubborn

Water Horse: Cheerful, intuitive, easily distracted

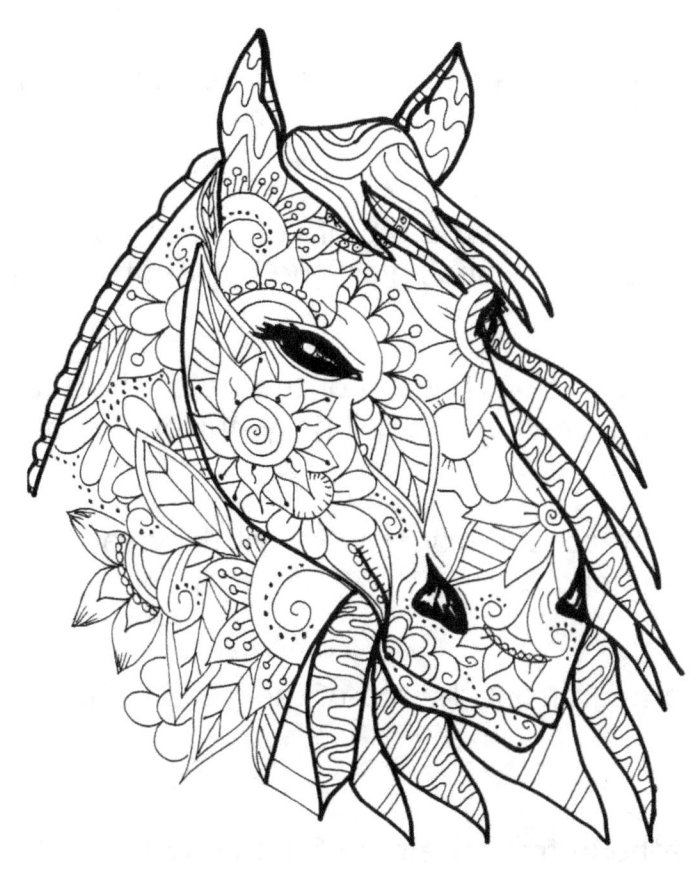

The Basics:

Fixed Season: Summer

Fixed Direction: South

Fixed Element: Fire

Associated Sun Sign: Gemini

Lucky Colour: brown, yellow, purple

Lucky Numbers: 2, 3, 7

Time of Day: 11am-1pm

Compatibility:

Good : Tiger, Sheep, Dog,

Bad : Monkey, Rooster, Pig

Chinese Zodiac Meditation

You could have someone read this to you slowly, record yourself and play it back or read it through and follow the process. You may choose to lie down or remain seated; whatever you decide allow yourself to be comfortable.

Let's begin to notice the largest sensation of breath in the body.

Allow this breath to expand to include the entire body.

Imagine sending your breath from the top of your head down to the tips of your toes.

Breathe from the top of your head to the knees. Send the breath back to the top of your head.....

Breathe from the top of your head down to your root (the groin area) and back to the top of your head....

Breathe in from the top of your head down to the second chakra, or energy center; located two inches below the belly button and back to the top of your head....

Breathe in from the top of the head down to the third chakra, or energy center; located two inches above the belly button and back to the top of your head....

Next breathe in from the top of the head down to the heart center and back to the top of the head....

Breathe in from the top of the head to the throat center and back to the top of the head....

Breathe in from the top of the head to the third eye point, the area on center of the forehead just above the brow, and back to the top of the head....

Feel the body sinking into a deeper state of relaxation. Allow the body to relax even more......

Relax the scalp and crown of the head…..

Relax your shoulders back and down from the ears……

Relax the upper cheeks, lower cheeks, jaw and tongue. Give the whole face permission to soften……

Relax your ears……

Relax the neck……

Relax the shoulders back and down, if seated, allow the elbows to dangle from the shoulder girdle. If lying down allow the elbows to relax……

Let the hands relax, fingers releasing to their natural curve……

Feel the breath rising and falling in the chest……

Feel the abdomen expand and collapse with the breath……

Let these sensations drop into the back side of the body and release the vertebrae; each one in turn from the cervical spine in the neck all the way down to the sacrum and coccyx……

Allow the hips to relax……

Release any tension in the thighs, your knees, the lower legs, ankles and feet……

Let any remaining tension release from the body from the tips of the toes……

So relaxed from the top of the head all the way down to the tips of the toes……

Any sounds you hear allow you to sink even deeper into a state of rest, of relaxation. As you bring the focus back to the third eye point located on the center of the brow…..

As we begin to take a mental journey.

See, sense, feel or imagine yourself outdoors at your favourite place in nature. A place where you feel content and at peace. The weather is absolutely perfect. The sun is shining. A soft breeze flows against your skin. Birds fly overhead. You can hear the sounds of wildlife surrounding you.

Off to the right you notice a path leading into a forest. Take this path. Notice the texture of the earth beneath your feet. Notice it's consistency; what is the pathway made of? Give it detail. Notice the slight temperature change as you move into the forest.

You can hear the sound of water flowing coming from somewhere up ahead. As you look, some 50 yards ahead of you, you can see a clearing.

Walk toward the clearing. As you grow closer still you feel droplets of water upon your face. And you know you have been guided toward a waterfall and a small river flowing from it's base.

As you view the crest of the waterfall you are able to see the sun shining brightly there. Find a place to sit near the waterfall. The surface of the water glitters and sparkles like diamonds. As you get comfortable you hear something off to the right.

You are not afraid…..

You turn to see your Zodiac Animal coming toward you.

It does not fear you. You smile. And begin to connect to the energy of your beloved Zodiac Animal.

It grows closer. You find yourself becoming even more still.

Some six feet away from you the animal stops for a rest. It looks at you with pure trust. And you welcome it into your heart. Slowly you blink your eyes at the being letting it know you too are not a source of fear but rather of universal connection.

The being seems to connect to a part of you so deep and infinite. And you begin to sense it's knowledge. It has secrets to share with you; things you are only now beginning to understand. This is your path, your journey to share the energy of this being.

It looks toward you and then toward the water. And you understand they are here to help you cleanse the body and mind of anything that is no longer serving you.

You carefully step into the warm water feeling the spray of the waterfall on your face.

As you watch the water it turns the most vibrant shade of red.
You allow this colour to fill you, to complete you, to make you whole.

After several minutes you notice the water shifting to a gorgeous shade of orange.
You allow this colour to fill you, to complete you, to make you whole.

After several minutes you notice the water shifting to a wonderful shade of yellow.
You allow this colour to fill you, to complete you, to make you whole.

After several minutes you notice the water shifting to a vibrant shade of green.
You allow this colour to fill you, to complete you, to make you whole.

Your Zodiac animal watches from a distance. And you know it is helping you to clear your physical body and mind. It supports you.

You look back to the water and notice it shifting in colour again this time to marvelous shade of blue.

You allow this colour to fill you, to complete you, to make you whole.

After several minutes you notice the water shifting now to Indigo; a beautiful mixture of purple-blue similar to a midnight sky.

You allow this colour to fill you, to complete you, to make you whole.

After several minutes you notice the water shifting to a breathtaking purple.

You allow this colour to fill you, to complete you, to make you whole.

From somewhere above you a gorgeous white light shines and begins to bathe your body. From head to toe your entire body begins to glow and you feel complete.

You step out of the water and make your way back to where you were sitting earlier. The sun has warmed the area and it feels so wonderful on your body. You look toward your zodiac animal. It is still there watching you. Feel it's love; your connection.   The animal begins to share information with you. Information about your current path in life. It tells you what you need to know in this moment.

You may hear words, see images, feel an attachment to them or connect to an inner sense of knowing. Listen to what they have to share…… (3-5 minutes of silence)

Now take the time to ask any questions you may have for clarification or to receive further understanding…(3-5 minutes of silence)

Thank the animal for sharing space with you. And return to the awareness to the present moment; knowing you can find your Zodiac animal whenever you choose as they are deeply connected with your heart.

Notes

About the Creator:

Tammy Lawrence-Cymbalisty is an Alternative Care provider working in the Kitchener/Waterloo Region. Since 2001 she has helped many people find peace, happiness, harmony and further purpose in their lives.

Tammy holds many degrees including: B.A. Sociology

(Trent University), Certified Yoga Teacher, Reiki

Master/Teacher, HypnoBirthing® Practitioner, Meditation Teacher, Workshop facilitator, Writer, Personal Growth Coach.

She lives with her husband, two felines and a school of fins in Cambridge, ON

Find out more by following Tammy on social media:

http://www.twitter.com/tllc

http://www.tinyurl.com/tlcservices

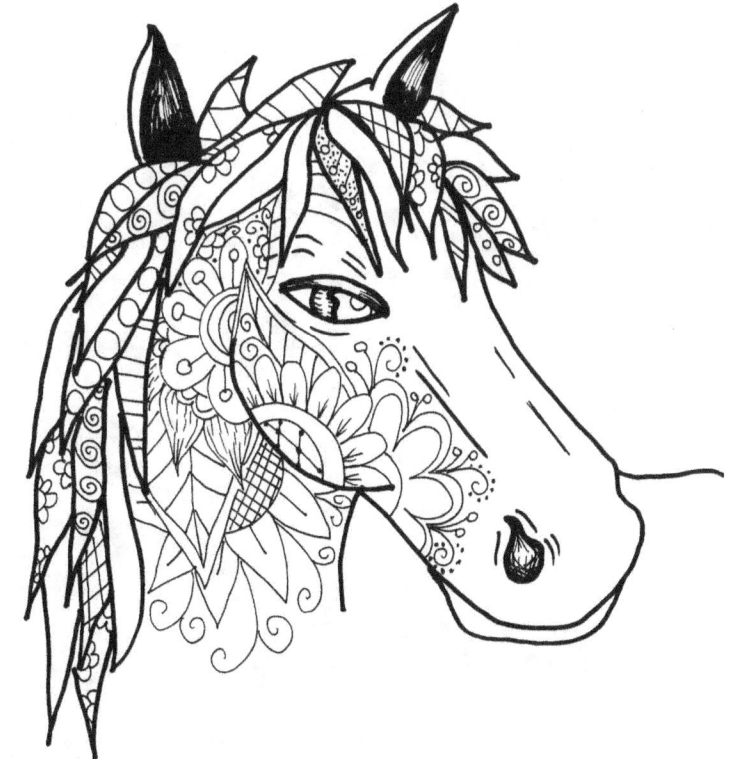

May you find peace

May you find happiness

May you be free from suffering

Namaste, Tammy

Be sure to purchase other colouring books designed & created by me!

Visit my Author Page: https://goo.gl/e387qf